Siri Hustvedt

Siri Hustvedt is the author of three novels: *The Blindfold*, *The Enchantment* of *Lily Dahl* and *What I Loved*. She has also published a book of poetry, *Reading to You*, and two collections of essays, *Yonder* and *The Mysteries of the Rectangle: Essays on Painting*. She lives in Brooklyn, New York.

Also by Siri Hustvedt

FICTION

The Blindfold

The Enchantment of Lily Dahl

What I Loved

NON-FICTION

Yonder

Mysteries of the Rectangle: Essays on Painting

POETRY

Reading to You

A Plea for Eros

Siri
Hustvedt

SCEPTRE

First published in Great Britain in 2006 by Hodder and Stoughton
A division of Hodder Headline

Essays in this collection have previously been published as follows:
'A Plea for Eros' in *Brick*, 1997, reprinted in *The Art of the Essay: The Best of
1999*, edited by Philip Lopate, Random House, 1999; 'Gatsby's *Glasses*'
in *Tributes: American Writers on American Writers, Conjunctions: 29*, 1997;
'Franklin Pangborn: An Apologia' in *O.K. You Mugs: Writers on Movie Actors*,
edited by Luc Sante and Melissa Pierson, Granta Books, 1999; 'Eight Days in a
Corset' in *Allure*, 1996; 'Living with Strangers' in the City Section of *The New
York Times*, 2002; 'The Bostonians: Personal and Impersonal Words' is an
introduction to the Barnes and Noble Classics edition of *The Bostonians*, 2005;
'Being a Man' in *Two Kingdoms: The Dualism Issues, Conjunctions: 41*, 2003; an
earlier version of 'One Year Later' in the *Observer*, 2002, and in *Die Zeit*
(Germany), 2002; 'Extracts from a Story of the Wounded Self' in *Samtiden*
(Norway), 2004; 'A Plea for Eros,' 'Yonder,' and 'Gatsby's *Glasses*' were published
in an earlier essay collection, *Yonder*, Henry Holt, 1998.

A Sceptre paperback

1

A CIP catalogue record for this title is available from the British Library

ISBN 0 340 83979 1

Typeset in Sabon by Palimpsest Book Production Limited,
Polmont, Stirlingshire
Printed and bound by Clays Ltd, St Ives plc

Hodder Headline's policy is to use papers that are natural, renewable
and recyclable products and made from wood grown in sustainable forests.
The logging and manufacturing processes are expected to conform to
the environmental regulations of the country of origin.

Hodder and Stoughton Ltd
A division of Hodder Headline
338 Euston Road
London NW1 3BH

For my mother,
Ester Vegan Hustvedt

Contents

Yonder

1

MY FATHER ONCE ASKED ME IF I KNEW WHERE YONDER WAS. I said I thought *yonder* was another word for *there*. He smiled and said, "No, yonder is between here and there." This little story has stayed with me for years as an example of linguistic magic: It identified a new space—a middle region that was neither here nor there—a place that simply didn't exist for me until it was given a name. During my father's brief explanation of the meaning of *yonder,* and every time I've thought of it since, a landscape appears in my mind: I am standing at the crest of a small hill looking down into an open valley where there is a single tree, and beyond it lies the horizon defined by a series of low mountains or hills. This dull but serviceable image returns when I think of *yonder,* one of those wonderful words I later discovered linguists call "shifters"—words distinct from others because they are animated by the speaker and move accordingly. In linguistic terms this means that you can never really find yourself *yonder.* Once you arrive at yonder tree, it becomes *here* and recedes forever into that imaginary horizon. Words that wobble attract me. The fact that *here* and *there* slide and slip depending on where I am is somehow poignant, revealing both the tenuous relation between words and things and the miraculous flexibility of language.

The truth is that what fascinates me is not so much being in a place as *not* being there: how places live in the mind once you have left them, how they are imagined before you arrive, or how they are seemingly called out of nothing to illustrate a thought or story like my tree down yonder. These mental spaces map our inner lives more fully than any "real" map, delineating the borders of here and there that also shape what we see in the present. My private geography, like most people's, excludes huge portions of the world. I have my own version of the famous Saul Steinberg map of the United States that shows a towering Manhattan; a shrunken, nearly invisible Midwest, South, and West; and ends in a more prominent California featuring Los Angeles. There have been only three important places in my life: Northfield, Minnesota, where I was born and grew up with my parents and three younger sisters; Norway, birthplace of my mother and my father's grandparents; and New York City, where I have now lived for the past seventeen years.

When I was a child, the map consisted of two regions only: Minnesota and Norway, my here and my there. And although each remained distinct from the other—Norway was far away across the ocean and Minnesota was immediate, visible, and articulated into the thousands of subdivisions that make up everyday geography—the two places intermingled in language. I spoke Norwegian before I spoke English. Literally my mother's tongue, Norwegian remains for me a language of childhood, of affection, of food, and of songs. I often feel its rhythms beneath my English thoughts and prose, and sometimes its vocabulary invades both. I spoke Norwegian first because my maternal grandmother came to stay in Northfield bright scholarship brought my father to the University of Oslo, where he met my mother. The details of how the two met are unknown to me. What is mythologized in some families was private in ours. My mother's sister once used the English expression "love at first sight" to describe that encounter, but I have never felt any reason to poke my nose into what is clearly their business. Oslo may not be Paris, but it's a lot bigger than Northfield and a lot less provincial, and when my mother traveled from one place to the other to marry my father, whose family she had never laid eyes on, she must have imagined the place that lay ahead. She must have seen in her mind a world my father had described at least in part to her, but whether that world tallied with what she actually found is another question altogether. What is certain is that she left a world behind her. As a child she lived in Mandal, the most southern city in Norway, and those years were by every account (not only my mother's) idyllic. Her memories from the first ten years of her life, with her parents, two brothers, and a sister in a beautiful house above the city where her father was postmaster, are ones of such aching happiness that she says she sometimes kept her memories from me and my three sisters in fear that we might feel deprived in comparison. When she was ten years old, her father lost his money and his land. He had undersigned a business deal for a relative that went sour. Although he might have saved himself from ruin, my grandfather kept his word of honor and paid on that debt, which wasn't really his, for the rest of his life. I think this event forms the greatest divide in my mother's life. Suddenly and irrevocably, it cut her off from the home she loved and threw her into another as surely as if the earth had opened up and formed an impassable chasm between the two. The family moved to Askim, outside of Oslo, and this is why my mother's voice carries traces of both a southern accent and an eastern one: the mingled sounds from either side of the chasm. I have never doubted the happiness of my mother's first ten years, in Mandal. She had parents who loved her, rocks and mountains and ocean just beyond her doorstep. There were maids to lighten housework, siblings and family close by, and Christmases celebrated hard and long at home and in the house of tante Andora and onkel Andreas, people I have imagined repeatedly but seen only in photographs taken when they were too young to have been the aunt and uncle my mother knew. But it seems to me that losing paradise makes it all the more radiant, not only for my mother but, strangely enough, for me. It is an odd but emotionally reso-nant coincidence that every time I have been in Mandal, it doesn't rain. Rain is the torment of all Norwegians, who seek the sun with a fervor that might look a little desperate to, say, a person from California. It rains a lot in Norway. But when my mother took us there in 1959, it was a summer of leg-endary sunshine, and when I was last in Mandal, for a family reunion in 1991 with my mother and sisters and my own daughter, the sun shone for days on end, and the city gleamed in the clear, perfect light of heaven.

I never knew my grandfather. He died when my mother was nineteen. There are photographs of him, one in which he stands facing a white horse with three young children on its back. He is wearing a straw hat that shades his eyes, and be-tween his lips is a cigarette. What is most striking in the pic-ture is his posture, proud and erect, but with another quality that is almost but not quite jaunty. It is somehow obvious that he didn't strike a pose. He had intelligent features—his eyes especially give the impression of thought. My grandmother said he read (almost to the exclusion of anything else) church history and Kierkegaard. She adored him and never married again. I'm sure it never entered her mind to do so. When I think of my mother's mother, I think of her voice, her gestures, and her touch. They were all soft, all refined; and, at the same time, she was freely and passionately affectionate. For some reason, I remember with tremendous clarity walking through her door, when I was twelve, with my sisters and my mother and father. It was winter and my mother had knit me a new white hat and scarf to go with my brown coat. When my grandmother greeted me, she put her hands on either side of my face and said, "You're so beautiful in white, my darling."

The last time I lived in Norway, I visited my grandmother every day after school. She lived in a tiny apartment that rose above a small, old graveyard in the city. She was always happy to see me. I'm afraid I was a morbidly serious adolescent that year, a girl who read Faulkner and Baldwin, Keats and Marx with equal reverence, and I must have been somewhat humorless company. But there was no one I liked being with more than her, and this may have made me livelier. We drank coffee. We talked. She loved Charles Dickens, whom she read in Norwegian. Years after she was dead, I wrote a dissertation on Dickens, and though my study of the great man would no doubt have alarmed her, I had a funny feeling that by taking on the English novelist I was returning to my Norwegian roots.

My *mormor* (in Norwegian maternal and paternal lines are distinguished: *mormor* literally means "mother-mother") is at the center of my real experiences of Norway, Norway as particular and daily, as one home. She was a *lady* in the old sense of the word, the word that corresponds to *gentleman*—a person who never shed her nineteenth-century heritage of gentility. I was deep in my self-righteous socialist phase, and I'll never forget her saying to me in her soft voice, "You must be the first person in the family to march in a May Day parade." She wore a hat and gloves every time she went out, dusted her impeccable apartment daily, including each and every picture frame that hung on the wall, and was shocked when her cleaning lady used the familiar form *du* when she spoke to her. I can recall her small apartment well: the elegant blue sofa, the pictures on the wall, the shining table, the birdcage that held her parakeet, Bitte Liten, a name I would translate as "the tiny one." And I remember every object with fierce affection. Had I not loved my grandmother, and had she not loved my mother very well and loved me, those things would just be things. After Mormor died, I walked with my own mother outside our house in Minnesota, and she said to me that the strangest part of her mother's death was that a person who had only wanted the best for her wasn't there anymore. I recall exactly where the two of us were standing in the yard when she said it. I remember the summer weather, the slight browning of the grass from the heat, the woods at our left. It's as if I inscribed her words into that particular landscape, and the funny thing is that they are still written there for me. Not long after that conversation, I dreamed that my grandmother was alive and spoke to me. I don't remember what she said in the dream, but it was one of those dreams in which you are conscious that the person is dead but is suddenly alive and with you again. Although all other architectural detail is lost, I know I was sitting in a room and my grandmother walked through a door toward me. It was a threshold dream, a spatial reversal of my memory of walking through her door and her telling me I was beautiful in white. I remember how intensely happy I was to see her.

My daughter, Sophie, has always called my mother "Mormor," and no name could be more evocative of the maternal line. *Mother-mother* is for me an incantation of pregnancy and birth itself, of one person coming from another, and then its repetition in time. When I was pregnant with Sophie, I felt it was the only time I had been physically plural—two in one. But of course it had happened before, when I was the one inside that first place. Uterine space is mysterious. We can't remember its liquid reality, but we know now that the fetus hears voices. After the violence of birth (all the classes, breathing, and birth-cult nonsense in the world do not make the event nonviolent), the newborn's recognition of his or her mother's voice forms a bridge across that first, brutal separation.

2

By its very nature, original space, maternal space, is nonsense; human experience there is undifferentiated and so can't be put into words. It lives on in our bodies, however, when we curl up to sleep, when we eat, when some of us bathe or swim. And surely it leaves its traces in our physical desire for another. Paternal space in an ideal sense is different. Although we are "of" our fathers, just as we are "of" our mothers, we were never "in" our fathers. Their separateness is obvious. In the real lives of real people, this distance may be exaggerated or diminished. A lot of children of my generation grew up with more or less absent fathers. I didn't. My father was very much *there* in my life and in the lives of my sisters, and like my mother, he was fundamentally shaped by the place where he grew up.

He was born in a log house in 1922, not far from Cannon

Falls, Minnesota. That house burned and the family moved close by, to the house where my grandparents lived throughout my childhood. That house never had plumbing, but there was a pump in the front yard. My sisters and I loved that rusty pump. I remember being so small I had to reach for the handle and then, using both hands and all my weight, I would pull down several times and wait for the gush of water. My father remembers a world of barn raisings, quilting bees, traveling peddlers, square dances, and sleighs pulled by horses. He attended a one-room schoolhouse, all grades together, and he was confirmed in Norwegian at Urland Church—a white wooden church with a steeple that stands at the top of a hill. For me, that church is a sign of proximity. When we reached the church in the family car, it meant we could spot my grandparents' house. The church was the last landmark in a series of landmarks, to which my sisters and I gave such inventive names as "the big hill." Every landmark was accompanied by an equally inventive song: "We are going down the big hill. We are going down the big hill." My parents were subjected to this for years. The trip was about seventeen miles and took about half an hour on the small roads. My sisters and I, like most children, were creatures of repetition and ritual. Places revisited were given a sacred and enchanted quality. I use those words carefully, because there was something liturgical about going over the same ground so many times. The products of both Lutheran Sunday school and fairy tales, we infused the places where we grew up with what we knew best.

Despite the fact that my parents shared a language, the worlds in which each of them grew up were very different. The Norwegian American immigrant communities formed in the Midwest in the nineteenth century and the country left behind were separated not only by miles but by culture. Those

"little Norways" developed very differently from the mother-
land, even linguistically. The dialects people brought with
them took another course on the prairie. English words with
no Norwegian equivalents were brought into spoken Norwegian and given gender. Norwegians who visited relations who
had lived in America for several generations were surprised
by their antiquated diction and grammar. The legacy of home-
steading, of primitive life on the prairie, along with the real
distance from the country of origin, kept the nineteenth century alive longer in America than in many parts of Norway.

My grandparents' small farm, reduced to twenty acres in
my lifetime, was our playground, but even as a child I sensed
the weight of the past, not only on that property, which was
no longer farmed, but in the community as a whole. I lived to
see it vanish. The old people are dead. Many of the little farms
have been sold and bought up by agribusinesses, and when
you walk into a store or visit a neighbor, people don't speak
Norwegian anymore. When my grandmother died, at ninety-
eight, my father spoke at her funeral. He called her "the last
pioneer." My father shuns all forms of cliché and false sentiment. He meant it. She was among the very last of the people
who remembered life on the prairie. My paternal grandmother, a feisty, outspoken, not entirely rational woman, especially when it came to politics, banks, and social issues,
could tell a good story. She had a swift and lean approach to
narrative that nevertheless included the apt, particular detail.
I often wish now I had recorded these stories on tape. When
she was six years old, Matilda Underdahl lost her mother. The
story, which became myth in our family, is this: When the local pastor told Tilly her mother's death was "God's will," she
stamped her foot and screamed, "No, it's not!" My grandmother retained a suspicion of religious pieties all her life.

She remembered the polio epidemic that killed many people she knew, and in a brief but vivid story, she made it real for me. She was sitting with her father at a window, watching two coffins being carried out of a neighboring house—one large and one small. As they watched, her father spoke to her in a low voice. "We must pray," he said, "and eat onions." She remembered a total eclipse of the sun, and she said she was told that the world was going to end. They dressed themselves in their Sunday clothes, sat down in the house, folded their hands, and waited. She remembered being told about the *nokken* in the well, a water monster that pulled little children down to the depths where it lived and probably ate them. Clearly meant to scare children from getting too close to the well and drowning, the story lured little Matilda straight to it. And there she tempted fate. She laid her head on the well's edge and let her long red curls dangle far down inside as she waited in stubborn, silent horror for the *nokken* to come.

But there is another small story I heard only once that has lasted in my mind. When she was a child, she lived near a lake in Minnesota in Otter Tail County; and during the winter, when that lake froze, she and the other children would take their sleds onto the lake and fit them out with sails. I can't remember what they used for sails, but when the wind was up, the sails would fill with air and propel the sleds across the ice, sometimes at great speed. When she told me this, her voice communicated her pleasure in this memory, and I saw those sleds from a distance, three or four on the wide expanse of a frozen lake gliding noiselessly across it. That is how I still imagine it. I don't see or hear the children. What she remembered is undoubtedly something so radically different from the image I gave to her memory that the two may be incompatible.

My great-grandfather on my mother's side was a sea captain. There is a painting of his ship that my uncle has now. She was called *Mars*. It may be that I have linked that painting of a great sailing ship on the ocean with the tiny ships on the ice in landlocked Minnesota, but I'm not sure. Tilly's family came from Underdahl in the Sogne Fjord. She never went there, but I saw Underdahl with my parents and sisters as we traveled by boat down the fjord where the mountainsides are so steep that farmers have traditionally used ladders to descend into the towns below. Underdahl has a tiny church. From the boat, the white structure looked almost doll-like, and the name for me has come to mean not only my grandmother but that miniature building.

The Depression hit my paternal grandparents hard. They weren't alone, of course, but my father's life was and is shaped by that hardship—of this I am certain. He has many stories about the people he grew up with, but his inner life and the pictures he carries with him, in particular the most painful ones, are hidden to me. I know that my father began working on other farms when he was ten years old. I know that my grandmother made and sold *lefse*, a flat potato cake, to bring in money. I know that there was a twelve-hundred-dollar debt on the farm that couldn't be paid once the Depression hit. Forty acres of the sixty-acre farm were lost. I know that after the United States entered the war my grandfather, like so many others, found work in a local defense plant. He was transferred to a town in Washington State and had to leave the family. He worked building the plant where the atomic bomb would later be manufactured. But he didn't know this until years later. Many people in that community worked themselves sick and silly, and their labor didn't prevent catastrophes of weather or economy, and people died of them—

physically and spiritually. It has become a truism to say that there was much that was unforgiving and brutal about that life, but it is nevertheless a fact, and by the time I saw the world where my father had lived as a child, a kind of stasis had set in. I remember how still my grandparents' farm was. The enormous sky and the flat fields and the absence of traffic on the road that ran past that place were only part of it. There was an inner stillness, too.

High in the mountains above the town of Voss, in western Norway, lies the farm that gave me my name: Hustveit. At some point, the *tveit* became *tvedt*, a different spelling for the same word, which means an opening or a clearing. I have been there. The place is now owned and cared for by the Norwegian government. You have to climb a mountain to reach Hustveit, and a landscape more different from the Minnesota prairie could hardly be imagined. I wondered what my great-grandfather saw when he imagined "Amerika." Could he have seen in his mind a landscape as open and flat as what he actually came to? Immigration inevitably involves error and revision. What I imagined it would be, it's not. For better or worse, some mistake is unavoidable.

My sisters and I loved to listen to a simple story about an immigrant's mistake in our own family. My grandfather's first cousin, whom my sisters and I called Uncle David, left Hustveit when he was twenty-two years old to make his way in America alone. He arrived at Ellis Island in August 1902. He spent his first day in New York City and was flabbergasted by the chaos, color, and crowds. Somewhere in the city, he saw a man selling apples, the most gorgeous, red, perfect apples he had ever seen. He had almost no money, but he lusted after one of those apples, and, overcome by desire, he splurged and bought one. The story goes that he lifted the apple to his mouth, bit into it, and spat it out in disgust. It was a tomato. Uncle David had never seen or heard of a tomato. My sisters and I roared with laughter at this story. It encapsulates so neatly the lesson of expectation and reality that it could serve as a parable. The fact that tomatoes are good is beside the point. If you think you're getting an apple, a tomato will revolt you. That New York should be nicknamed the Big Apple, that an apple is the fruit of humankind's first error and the expulsion from paradise, that America and paradise have been linked and confused ever since Europeans first hit its shores, makes the story reverberate as myth.

On the other hand, if not violently overthrown, expectation can have a power in itself, can invest a place with what literally isn't there. When I saw Hustveit, I felt the same reverence I felt the last time I was in Mandal. They are both beautiful places, it is true, the stuff of postcards and nineteenth-century landscape painting, but no doubt I would have felt reverent in less lovely places, because I imagined a past I connected to myself. Walking beside my mother up toward the house where she lived with her parents and siblings, I imagined what she must have felt walking over that ground where she walked as a child, remembering people now dead, especially her father and her mother, and that empathy provoked in me deep feeling. My father never lived at Hustveit, nor did his father, but it was a strong presence in both their lives. In 1961, out of the blue, my grandfather Lars Hustvedt inherited 5,850 crowns, about 850 dollars, from a Norwegian relative, Anna Hustveit. He used the money to travel to Norway for the first and last time, visiting Voss and Hustveit during the trip. He was seventy-four years old. My grandfather's sojourn in Norway was a great success. According to my father, he impressed his relatives with his intimate knowledge of Hustveit.

w exactly where every building on the property lay and
what it looked like from his father, who had described his
birthplace in detail to his son. Hustveit was and is a real
place, but it is also a sign of origin. I don't doubt that there
were times when that sign alone, carried from one generation
to another in a name, accompanied by a mental image, anchored the people who had left it and anchored their children
and grandchildren as well in another place, crushed by the vi-
cissitudes of nature and politics.

My grandfather remembered what he had never seen. He
remembered it through someone else. It is no doubt a tribute
to his character and to his father's that the image handed
down from one to the other seems to have been remarkably
accurate. Every story is given some kind of mental ground.
The expression "I see" in English for "I understand" is hardly
haphazard. We are always providing pictures for what we
hear. My mother and father both lived through World War II,
my mother in occupied Norway and my father as a soldier in
New Guinea, the Philippines, and finally Japan during the occupation. They were both inside that immense historical cata-
clysm. Each has a story of how it began, and I like both of
them, because they are oddly parallel. In the middle of the
first semester of his freshman year at St. Olaf College (the college where he would later become a professor and where
three of his four daughters would be students), he was sitting
at a table covered with index cards, on which he had tirelessly
recorded the needed information for a term paper he was
struggling to write, when his draft notice arrived in the mail.
My father told me his first response was: "Great! Now I don't
have to finish this damned paper." Reading his draft notice,
my father didn't look mortality in the face. That would come
later. My mother told me that the morning after the Nazi in-

vasion of Norway, April 9, 1940, my grandmother woke up her children by saying, "Get up. It's war." Rather than fear, my mother felt only intense excitement. I have given both of these stories settings in my mind. When I think of my father and his index cards, I see him in a college house where a friend of mine lived when I was a student. It's a false setting. My father didn't live there. I needed a place and I plopped him down in that house unconsciously. I never saw where my mother lived during the war either, but I see my grandmother waking her children in rooms I've cooked up to fill the emptiness. I see morning light through the windows and a white bed where my mother opens her eyes to discover that the German army is on Norwegian soil.

Both of my mother's brothers were in the Norwegian Underground, and I have given their stories settings, too. Neither one of them ever said a word about their involvement, but my mother told me that one day she saw her brother Sverre talking to the schoolteacher in town and she knew. I see my uncle near a brick building speaking to a short, balding man. My mother never provided these details. They're my own, and I'm sure they're wrong, but the image persists. I have never changed or embellished it in any way. Later in the war, my uncle Sverre got word that the Nazis had been informed of his Underground involvement, and he skied to Sweden to escape. He spent the remaining years of the war there. My mother and her sister took him into the woods and waved good-bye. Again, not a word about where he was going was ever spoken. I see the three of them in the snow among bare trees, a few brown stalks protruding from the snow. My uncle has a backpack and he skis off, propelling himself forward briskly with his poles. Often the origins of such images are untraceable, but sometimes the associative logic at work announces itself after a moment's thought. The chances that the building near which my mother's brother stood was brick are unlikely. The red brick in my mind is conjured from the word *schoolteacher*. All my schools were brick.

And sometimes a detail provided by the teller grows in the mind of the listener, as is the case with potatoes in a story my mother told me. She was jailed by the Germans in Norway for nine days in February after the April invasion. She and a number of other students had protested the occupation in December. Nazi officers came to her school and arrested her. Rather than pay a fine, she chose jail. As my mother has often said, had it been later, the protesters would have been sent to Germany and would probably never have returned; but as she also always adds, had it been later, nobody would have dared protest openly. When I was a child, the idea of my dear, pretty mother in jail filled me with both indignation and pride. My sisters and I were the only children we knew of in Northfield who could boast of having a mother who had been in "jail." She was in a tiny cell with a single high-barred window, a cot, and a pail for urine and feces—just like in the movies. The food was bad. She told me the potatoes were green through and through. Those potatoes loom in my mind as the signifier of that jail. When I imagine it, everything is in black-and-white like a photograph, except the potatoes, which glow green in the dim light. After only nine days, she left jail with a bloated stomach.

My father has talked very little about the war. He once said to me that he kept himself sane by telling himself over and over that the whole thing was insane. One story he told me left a deep impression. While he was a soldier in the Philippines, he became ill, so ill that he was finally moved to a collecting station. His memory of those days is vague, because his fever was high and he passed in and out of consciousness. At the station, however, he woke up and noticed a tag on his chest that said YELLOW FEVER. He had been misdiagnosed. I have always imagined this memory of my father's as if I were my father. I open my eyes and try to orient myself. I am lying on a cot in a makeshift hospital outside, along with other maimed and sick soldiers on stretchers. The tag is yellow. This transfer of the name of the illness onto the tag is, I'm sure, ludicrous, but my brain is obviously in the business of bald simplification, and that's how I see it. This scene takes place in color. I have certainly borrowed its details from war movies and from what I have seen of Asia, not where my father found himself but farther north, in Thailand and China.

Why I imagine myself inside my father's body in this story and not inside my mother's body when she was jailed is not, I think, accidental. It corresponds to the distinct levels of consciousness in each story—that is, in order to understand what happened to my mother, it is enough to move myself into that jail and see her there. In order to understand what happened to my father, I must imagine waking in a fever and making out the letters that spell imminent death. I rechecked this story with my father, and he says there was no yellow fever in the Philippines then and he really doesn't know who made the diagnosis. In reality, he, not the tag, was yellow. He suffered from severe jaundice, a result of having both malaria and hepatitis. Because my father has never shared the other stories, the horrors of combat itself, this experience became for me the quintessential moment of war, a tale of looking at one's own death. It can be argued that accuracy isn't always crucial to understanding. I have never been in jail and I have never been a soldier, but I imagined these events and places to the extent that it is possible for me, and that imagining has brought me closer to my parents.

After the war, my father finished St. Olaf College on the GI Bill, with a lot of other vets who are now legend in the history of the school. A college started by Norwegian immigrants and affiliated with the American Lutheran Church, St. Olaf attracts the mostly well-behaved offspring of white middle-class midwesterners, many of them with Norwegian roots. It is not a wild place. Dancing was forbidden until the 1950s. I went to college there, had some wonderful teachers, but the students were by and large a sleepy, complacent lot, more conservative than their professors and easily "managed" by them. My father and his veteran cohorts were not. He tells a story about a man I knew as somebody's highly respectable "dad" literally swinging from the rafters in one of the dormitories. I see him flying above a crowd of heads with a bottle of whiskey. The bottle, however, may well be my embellishment. Four years at war had turned them into men, as the saying goes, and they took the place by storm, not only with their poker games and Tarzan antics but with their intellectual hunger. All this is true, and yet it has taken on the quality of fiction. I read the stories I've been told in my own way and make a narrative of them. Narrative is a chain of links, and I link furiously, merrily hurdling over holes, gaps, and secrets. Nevertheless, I try to remind myself that the holes are there. They are always there, not only in the lives of others but in my own life as well.

The stories and pictures I make for the lives of the people closest to me are the forms of my empathy. My father took the place he knew best and transfigured it, but he has never left it behind. He received his Ph.D. in Scandinavian studies from the University of Wisconsin at Madison. His dissertation,

which became a book and was awarded the McKnight Prize
for literature, is a biography of Rasmus Bjørn Andersen—an
influential figure in the Norwegian American immigrant community. The book is not only the biography of a man but the
story of a time and place. My father has used his gifts to understand and preserve "home," not in the narrow sense of that
single house with those particular people but in its larger
sense of subculture. I think it is fair to argue that his "place"—
the world of his childhood, the world I glimpsed in the old
people I knew as a child—is now paper. My father has been
the secretary of the Norwegian American Historical Association for over thirty years. The association publishes books
about immigrant history, but it is also an archive. Over the
years, my father has devoted countless hours to organizing
what was once unsorted mountains of paper in innumerable
boxes and is now an annotated archive of letters, newspapers,
diaries, journals, and more. These are facts. What is more interesting is his will to do it, his tireless commitment to the
work of piecing together a past. Simple nationalism or chauvinism for a "people" is beside the point. The archive provides
information on fools as well as on heroes; it documents both
hardy pioneers and those who died or went mad from home-
sickness. There is a story of a farmer who thought the flatness
of the Minnesota land would kill him if he looked at it any
longer; unearthing rock after rock, he built his own mountain
in memory of the home he had left. My mother felt a natural
sympathy for this man, and when a huge rock was dug out of
her own yard in Minnesota, she kept it. It's still there—her
"Norwegian mountain." When I worked with my father on the
annotated bibliography of that archive, I began to understand
that his life's work has been the recovery of a place through
the cataloging of its particularity—a job that resembles, at

least in spirit, the Encyclopedists of the eighteenth century. By its very nature, the catalog dignifies every entry, be it a political tract, a letter, or a cake recipe. Though not necessarily equal in importance, each is part of the story, and there's a democracy to the telling, I think, too, although my father has never told me this, that his work has been for his own father, an act of love through the recovery of place and story.

I remember my grandfather as soft-spoken and, as with my grandmother on my mother's side, I remember his touch. It struck me, even as a child, as unusually tender. There was no brusqueness in him, and I remember that when I showed him my drawings his sober, quiet face would come alive. He chewed tobacco, and he offered us ribbon candy as a special treat. He lost four fingers to an axe chopping wood, and I recall that the stubs on his hand fascinated but didn't scare me. When I think of him, I remember him in a particular chair in the small living room of his house. He died of a stroke the year I was in Norway: 1973. I was too far away to attend the funeral. We were not a long-distance-telephone family. They wrote me the news. I spoke to my parents once that year on the phone.

3

My first real memory takes place in a bathroom. I remember the tile floor, which is pale, but I can't give it a color. I am walking through the door toward my mother, who is in the bath. I can see the bubbles. I know it's a real memory and not a false one taken from photographs or stories because there are no pictures of that bathroom and because the proportions of the bathtub and toilet correspond to the height of a small person. The bubbles fascinate me, and the presence of my mother fills me with strong, simple pleasure. My mother, who hasn't spent much time in bubble baths during the course of her life, has always been somewhat dubious about this memory. But within this isolated fragment I see the path of my walk—the hallway, the small living area, the door to the kitchen; and when I described the walk to my mother, she confirmed that the rooms correspond to the graduate-student barracks near the University of Wisconsin at Madison. I was three.

I have memories of that first trip to Norway, too. The most striking is one of light and color. I am sitting outside at a table with my sister and my mother and my aunt. My cousins were probably there as well, but I have no memory of them. The sunshine is so brilliant I have to squint. We are close to water. I have no idea whether it was a fjord near Bergen or the ocean off Mandal. It's water and it's blue. It's probably the fjord, because I do not remember vastness or a beach but trees and rocks. The table is white, and on the table are glasses of shining soda pop—yellow and red. Those glasses of *brus* (the Norwegian word for soda pop, a word I never forgot) delight and fascinate me. I am quite sure that I'd never seen red soda before, and the memory is so powerful, I must have felt I was in the presence of a Norwegian miracle. That bottle of red *brus* on a white table gleamed throughout the remaining years of my childhood as the sign of what was possible *there*. It may have been in part responsible for the question I asked my mother when I was five or six: "Why is everything better in Norway?" I don't remember asking the question, but my mother assures me I was tactless enough to ask it. My poor mother decided that she had framed her emigration in the wrong light and vowed to be more careful about her comparisons between the two countries in the future.

Early memories are isolated bits of experience remembered for reasons that are often difficult to articulate; and because they have no greater narrative in which they can be framed, they float. At the same time, they may have more purity than later memories, for that very reason. When dailiness enters memory, repetition fixes places in the mind, but it also burdens them with a wealth of experience that is often difficult to untangle. For example, I remember Longfellow School, where I attended grade school, very well. I can see its hallways and connect one to another. I can even see the bathroom outside my third-grade class. I remember it as gray. It may have been gray, but it could be that I colored it in memory. I have given the interior of that building a single color that is also emotional: gray. Although I was always excited to begin school in the fall (a season separated from the spring before by years of summer), and although I loved walking out to the school bus with my three sisters, all of us wearing the identical new dresses my mother had sewn for us, my memory of the school building itself, its rooms and lockers, blackboards, and hallways, brings on a heavy, oppressive feeling. Whether I was more unhappy in school than any of my friends I don't know. I never would have said I didn't like school, and there are moments I distinctly remember enjoying, but these truths don't alter my memory of that place. There's something unpleasant about saying that a gut response can be a lie, but I think it's possible. Unlike the intricacy of the physical world, feelings are generally more crude than language—guilt, shame, being hurt by another person feel remarkably alike in the body. Reason tells me that my early experiences in that school were a complex mixture of pain, pleasure, and boredom, but whenever I drive past it or think about it, the building itself is wrapped in gloom.

Many years later, I had a similar experience but in reverse. From 1978 through 1986, I was a graduate student at Columbia, but by 1981 I had met my future husband and moved first to SoHo, in downtown Manhattan, and then to Brooklyn. It is true that those first couple of years, when I was living near Columbia, I was very poor. It is true that I suffered in a difficult and stupid love affair and that I worked at one bad job after another to try to keep myself going. Nevertheless, I remember that time as extraordinary, and I wouldn't trade it for anything. I don't even wish now that I had had more money. And had I been asked if I was suffering at the time, I would have said a defiant *no*. After I left that neighborhood, however, I rarely returned to it. I saw my dissertation adviser three times in three years and then defended on a clear spring day in 1986. After that, I disappeared for good. Several years later, I returned, because my husband, Paul Auster, had been asked to give a talk at the Maison Française. Walking across campus made me feel sad, and I thought to myself, I wasn't happy here. Then, after the reading, we walked past Butler Library. It was dark, but the light inside illuminated the windows. Students were reading and working, and those lit windows gave me a wonderful, weightless feeling. I understood for the first time how happy I had been there—in the library. Butler is a good library, one of the best. It has some handsome rooms, but its stacks are inhospitable and dark. One spring while I was a student, all the women were given whistles before they entered the stacks, because an exhibitionist had been prowling the badly lit corridors, and we were told to pucker up and blow if there was any trouble. Again, I don't fully understand my emotional response to that library or trust it. It was the site of a series of intellectual revelations that were crucial to me, not just as a student but as a human being. I read Sigmund Freud in that library and Émile Benveniste and Roman Jakobson and Mikhail Bakhtin and was forever changed by them, but I also sweated out bad papers and was bored and troubled and irritated there. My mind wandered from the work at hand and strayed to food or clothes I couldn't afford or to the attractive arms and shoulders of some young man sitting at the far end of the table. So what does it mean that the sight of Butler Library turned me into a quivering heap of sentimental mush? It can only be that places left behind often become emotionally simplified—that they sound a single note of pain or pleasure, which means that they are never what they were.

At the same time, I'm fully aware that libraries occupy a particular place in my life, and my sudden burst of feeling for Butler isn't related only to my life as a graduate student. My father took me and my sisters into the dim, dusty stacks on the seventh floor of Rolvaag Library at St. Olaf, where he worked for the historical association. To get there, we walked into an old elevator with a bright red door and a grate that folded and unfolded with lots of creaking and banging. I was already a heroine then, Alice or Pollyanna or a generic princess from a fairy tale—and the trip into that landscape of book spines and bad light made me feel like a person in a story on some curious adventure. It may be that I link every library to that first one—to my early childhood experience of drawing on the floor near my father's desk. A library is of course a real place, but it is also an unreal one. What happens there is mostly silent. I think I've always liked the whispering aspect of libraries, the hushing librarians and my feeling of solitude among many. When her children were older, my mother worked part-time in the St. Olaf library, too. She was employed there when I was a student. I didn't sleep in Rolvaag Library, but most of my waking hours were spent in a carrel there, and sometimes she would come to see me. I would feel her hands on my shoulders and turn my head, knowing I was going to see my mother. Years before she found herself filing periodicals in that library, she found books for me. It was my Norwegian mother, not my American father, who introduced me to the English poems and novels that affected me most when I was young. She gave me Blake's *Songs of Innocence and Experience* when I was eleven. I didn't understand those poems, but they fascinated me as much as *Alice in Wonderland* had, and I read them again and again with mingled horror and pleasure. She gave me Emily Dickinson, too, around the same time, a tiny green edition of famous poems, and I would repeat those poems to myself in a trance. They were secrets to me, strange and private. I think it was the sound of those poems that I loved. I chewed on Blake's and Dickinson's words like food. I ate them, even when their meanings eluded me.

It was my mother who sent me off to the library for *David Copperfield* and *Jane Eyre* and *Wuthering Heights* when I was thirteen, and it's fair to say that to this day I have not recovered from a single one of those novels. That was the summer of 1968, and my family was in Iceland. I cannot think of Reykjavik without the thought that I was David and Jane and Catherine there in that house, where I found it hard to sleep, because the sun never set. I would go to the window and lift the shade in the bedroom and look out into the eerie light that fell over the roofs, not daylight at all, some other light I had never seen before and have never seen since. The other-worldly landscape of Iceland has come to mean story for me.

My father took us out into the countryside to the places where the sagas are said to have taken place. The sagas are fiction, but their settings are geographically exact. My father stopped the Volkswagen Bug we had rented; and after all six of us had piled out of that tiny car, and we stood on that treeless ground with its black lava rock and smoking geysers and green lichen, my father showed us where Snorre died. "The axe fell on him here!" And when my father said it, I saw the blood running on the ground. When he wasn't finding the sites where the heroes had wandered, my father was in the library reading about them. The very idea of a library for me is bound to my mother and father and includes the history of my own metamorphoses through books, fictions that are no less part of me than much of my own history.

4

Seventy-six years after Uncle David walked off the ship at Ellis Island, I arrived at the airport in New York City. It was early September 1978. I didn't know a living soul in the place. My suitcase was heavy, and nobody helped me carry it, something unheard of in Minneapolis. But frankly, even this indifference from New Yorkers didn't bother me. I had left small-town, rural life for good, and I had no intention of ever returning, not because I didn't like my home but because I had always known that I would leave. Leaving was part of my life romance, part of an idea I had about myself as a person destined for adventure; and as far as I could tell, adventure lay in the urban wilds of Manhattan, not in the farmland of Minnesota. This was my guiding fiction, and I was determined to make good on it. I had a tiny room in International House, on West 123rd Street at Harlem's border. My first three days were spent rereading *Crime and Punishment* in a state that closely resembled fever. I couldn't sleep, because the noise from traffic, sirens, garbage trucks, and exuberant pedestrians outside my window kept me wide awake all night. I had no friends. Was I happy? I was wildly happy. Sitting on my bed, which took up most of the space in that narrow room, I whispered prayers of thanks that I was really and truly *here* in New York, beginning another life. I worshipped the place. I feasted on every beautiful inch of it—the crowds, the fruit and vegetable stands, the miles of pavement, the graffiti, even the garbage. All of it sent me into paroxysms of joy. Needless to say, my elation had an irrational cast to it. Had I not arrived laden with ideas of urban paradise, I might have felt bad losing sleep, might have felt lonely and disoriented, but instead I walked around town like a love-struck idiot, inhaling the difference between *there* and *here*. I had never seen anything like New York, and its newness held the promise of my future: dense with the experience I craved—romantic, urbane, intellectual. Looking back on that moment, I believe I was saved from disappointment by the nature of my "great expectations." I honestly wasn't burdened with conventional notions of finding security or happiness. At that time of my life, even when I was "happy," it wasn't because I expected it. That was for characters less romantic than myself. I didn't expect to be rich, well fed, and kindly treated by all. I wanted to live deeply and fully, to embrace whatever the city held for me, and if this meant a few emotional bruises, even a couple of shocks, if it meant not eating too well or too often, if it meant a whole slew of awful jobs, so be it.

It appears that time has turned that young woman, who

imagined herself a romantic heroine, into something of a comic character, but I remain fond of her. We are relatives, after all. Like all the places where I've actually lived, New York City is much more than a "context" or "setting" for me. Within weeks of my arrival in New York, I was someone else, not because there had been a revolution in my psychological makeup or any trauma. It was simply this: people saw me in a light in which I had never been seen before. Although I had always felt at home with my parents and sisters, I was never really comfortable with my peers. By the time I found myself in college, my feeling that I was not inside but outside had intensified. There's no question that I cultivated this to some degree, that I prided myself on my difference, but I confess it hurt and surprised me to be regarded as "strange." I had friends I loved and teachers I loved, but rumors in which I was variously characterized as wild, monkishly studious, or just plain weird haunted my career as a college student. I recall my father telling me with a smile that one of his students had described me as "very unique." In New York, this all but ended. Whatever exoticism I may have possessed came from my midwestern sincerity and lack of worldly sophistication. Transformations of the self are related to *where* you are, and identity *is* dependent on others. In Minnesota, I felt embattled. I rebelled against a culture that touted "niceness" above truth, that wallowed in an idea of "equality" that had come to mean "sameness" and "intolerance"—not of the sick, dying, ugly, or handicapped but of those who distinguished themselves by talent or beauty or intelligence. The "hoity-toity" were really batted around out there. Pretension wasn't suffered for an instant, and for a girl who walked around dreaming she was a combination of George Eliot and Nora Charles in *The Thin Man*, life could be hard. In Minnesota, I lusted after every quality that was in short supply—artifice, irony, flamboyant theatricality, fierce intellectual debate, and brilliantly painted lips.

In New York, "niceness" wasn't an overriding value, but then neither was "goodness," a value I frankly and unashamedly clung to for dear life. I had to reorient myself to accommodate a new world. For example, I naïvely assumed that most people had had some kind of religious education, that religion remained a fact of most people's lives and provided the ground for moral life. I was startled to discover, however, when we were assigned the first book of the Bible for a literature class, that a majority of my fellow students had never read Genesis. Nevertheless, I wasn't an "odd duck" in New York, the city that accommodates or ignores all ducks. And despite the harshness of everyday life—the raw, cold, scraping sensation of never leaving the street, because my apartment felt as if it were *in* the street—I was at home in New York. This feeling of being "home at last" corresponds to my idea about the city, an idea shaped by books, movies, and plays, an idea of infinite possibility.

There is an incident, however, that made me understand what New York is for the people who come here to stay. I had been living in Manhattan for two years. I had met my future husband, and we were invited to a dinner at Westbeth—the housing project in the West Village for artists. I was delighted to be there in that company. I was in love. I was happy without having sought happiness. I vaguely remember wearing something silly, but no one minded. Everyone at the table looked like a marvel to me, but there was one man in particular who shone that night. It seemed to me that he had stepped right out of a Noël Coward play. His jokes were witty, his repartee sharp, and his manner nonchalant. He had written a book on Andy Warhol—no surprise. He was the most urbane creature I had ever laid eyes on. And I laughed and smiled and felt like Miranda: "How beauteous mankind is. O brave new world that has such people in't." The conversation wandered, as conversations do, and people began to talk about where they had grown up. Nobody, if I remember correctly, had been born and raised in New York City, and where had my idol sprung from, this divinity of culture and wit? Where had he spent his entire childhood and youth? In Northfield, Minnesota. I hadn't known him, because he is several years older than I am, but there it was: he and I had grown up in the same small town. New York City is the place where people come to invent, reinvent, or find the room they need to be who they wish to be. It's a place where fictions run freely and plentifully, where people are allowed a certain pretense about themselves, where cultivating a persona or an idea of how to live is permitted, even encouraged. This is the glory of urban freedom and indifference. It has its drawbacks, of course. One summer I was alone in New York. All my friends had fled the city heat, and I remember thinking, If I died right now in my apartment, how long would it take before anybody noticed?

I now live in Brooklyn, the place that nobody visits but where many people live. It is more ethnically diverse than Manhattan. The buildings are lower. We have more trees. I have zealously attached myself to my neighborhood, Park Slope, and defend it loyally. But all the time I've lived in Brooklyn, I've been writing about other places. I wrote a book called *The Blindfold* here, about a young graduate student who lives near Columbia and has a number of peculiar adventures. She and I aren't the same person, but she's close to me. And I put her in my old apartment, the one I rented on West 109th Street. When I wrote her stories, I saw her in my apartment and on the streets I knew so well. What she did wasn't what I had done, but I don't think I could have written that book had I not put her there, and I couldn't have written it had I still been living in that building.

5

Long before I had heard about the New Critics or structural-ism or deconstruction, teachers liked to talk about "setting" as one of the elements of fiction. It went along with "theme" and "character." I can't remember how Paul and I started our dis-cussion of place in fiction or how we arrived at his startling comment about *Pride and Prejudice*. But I clearly remember him saying that Austen's novel had taken place in his parents' living room in New Jersey. Although any self-respecting ju-nior high school teacher would have scoffed at such a remark about "setting," I realized I had done the same thing while reading Céline's novel *Death on the Installment Plan*. When Ferdinand finally takes refuge in his uncle's house, I imagined him in my paternal grandparents' little white house outside of Cannon Falls. Ferdinand says, "Yes, Uncle," in the small bed-room on the ground floor off the living room. The disparities between a gentry drawing room in England in the late eigh-teenth century and a suburban living room in New Jersey in the middle of the twentieth, or the ones between the French countryside in the early part of this century and the rural Midwest, are plain. What is remarkable to me is that I had to think about it to know what I had done. When you read, you see. The images aren't manufactured with effort. They simply appear to you through the experience of the text and are rarely questioned. The pictures conjured are enough to push you forward and are to a large extent, I think, like my image of the word *yonder*. They serve a function. And like the picture I carry with me of my uncle talking to his colleague in the Underground, they are not fully fleshed out. Although I can imagine my uncle's face because I knew him when he was alive, the schoolteacher is a blur except for his bald head.

Fictional characters are not constantly trampling over home territory in my mind, however. Often the source of the image is less clear. *Middlemarch* is a book I've read several times, and when Dorothea is in Rome with Casaubon, I always have the same picture of it. This is significant, because I read the book both before and after I actually visited Rome, and the real city didn't disturb in any way the imaginary one I had provided for Dorothea. Eliot's Rome in *Middlemarch* is for me essentially a stage set. The walls of the empty and dead city are built of cardboard that has been painted to look like stone. While the image is wrongheaded in some way, what I see is architecture as metaphor. Dorothea's terrible mistake is that she sees truth and power in what is false and impotent, and my artificial Rome extends the discovery of her wedding trip to the city where it occurs. Every time I read anything, I loot the world with luxurious abandon, robbing from real places and unreal ones, snatching images from movies, from postcards and paintings and even cartoons. And when I think of a book, especially one that is dear to me, I see those stolen places again, and they move me. There is a reason, after all, why Paul imagined the elaborate social intercourse and moral drama of Austen in his parents' living room. It was clearly the site for him of similar exchanges. Things happened in that living room. As for why Ferdinand's final refuge in the country belongs to my grandparents' house, it is for me the place of my father, and after that poor boy's ridiculous and heart-breaking adventures, he finds comfort at last from a paternal figure—his uncle.

The place of reading is a kind of yonder world, a place that is neither here nor there but made up of the bits and pieces of experience in every sense, both real and fictional, two categories that become harder to separate the more you think about them. When I was doing research for a professor as a graduate student, a job that paid my tuition and fees, I read excerpts from diaries recorded during Captain Cook's legendary voyages. On the expedition, both captain and crew saw a volcano. This volcano was described separately by Cook himself and by a young man aboard ship. The difference between those descriptions astonished me. Cook reports on the volcano in the cool, scientific prose of the Enlightenment, but the young man describes the same sight in rapturous tones already coded by Romanticism. The two looked in the same direction, but they didn't see the same event. Each had his own language for seeing, and that language created his vision. We all inherit vision just as they did—two men who stood side by side but were nevertheless separated by an intellectual chasm. It is almost impossible for us as residents of the Western world to imagine a pre-Romantic view of nature. My feeling for mountainous western Norway, undoubtedly shaped by the history of my family there, is also influenced by Romanticism. People simply don't see mountains as annoying impasses anymore. They breathe in the air and beat their breasts and drink in the beauty of the rugged landscape, but where does this come from, if not from the Romantics, who took up crags and cliffs as the shape of the sublime? No place is naked. It may be that in infancy we experience the nakedness of place, but without memory it remains inaccessible.

After my daughter was born, I flew around the apartment where I lived, in the grip of a new mother's euphoria. I couldn't look at my darling's tiny face enough, couldn't see it enough, and I had to creep into her room when she napped just to stare down at her in stupefied awe. But when I looked at her, I often wondered what the world was like from her point of view. She didn't know where she began or ended, didn't know that the toes she found so entertaining belonged to her. But connections come fast for babies. Meanings are made early through the presence and absence of the mother, through the cry answered, the smile answered, through sounds that are not language but like language, and then words themselves appear as a response to what is missing. Now that she's eight, Sophie lives in a world so dense with shaping fictions that her father and I are continually amused. She's a poor woman with a scarf around her head and a begging cup. She's a country-and-western singer, drawling out lyrics about lost love. She's Judy Garland in an obscure musical called *Summer Stock*. She's Pippi. She's Anne of Green Gables. She's a mother with a vengeance, changing, burping, waking the angel from naps, cooing and singing and patting and strolling her. The "baby" is life-size, plastic, and made in France.

For all the radical persona experimentation we call "play," children are placemongers. More than adults, they like to stay put, and they like order in the form of repetition. They attach themselves fiercely to houses, rooms, and familiar objects, and change is frowned upon. The son of a close friend of Paul's and mine is a case in point. For years he lived with his painter father in a loft in downtown Manhattan. The bathroom in their loft was a sad affair with broken flooring. When the father started earning more money from his work, he renovated the bathroom. His son mourned. "That old bathroom floor was my friend." Parents often discover that their redecorating schemes are anathema to their children. My daughter has moved just once in her eight years, from a small apartment in Brooklyn to a large brownstone a block and a half away. When we showed her the new house, she didn't like it. She worried about the strange furniture in it. I think she imagined that the people from whom we bought the house would leave their things, and all those unfamiliar objects made her uncomfortable. Then she had to survive the painting of the house, including her room, which took a couple of weeks, and she didn't like that either. But once she had settled herself there and had arranged her toys, she glued herself to that place and has invested it with all the affection she felt for her old room. The power of forms—spatial and verbal—as needed orientation in life can hardly be overestimated.

And every night I read to her. We have made our way through innumerable books, all fourteen *Oz* books, five *Anne* books, the Narnia series, all the Moomintroll books, E. Nesbitt and Lloyd Alexander and fairy tales from all over the world. Reading is a ritual that is itself associated with place, an event that happens after her teeth have been brushed and before she sleeps. No matter how harrowing the tales or how deep the identification (Sophie gasps, shudders, and, on occasion, sobs loudly during our reading), her body at least is securely in its bed. It may be that the singularity of place within the ritual is exactly what makes the sadness, fear, and excitement of these stories not only bearable but pleasurable. Repetition within ritual creates order through time, comes closer to the truth. Children, especially, long for wholeness, for unity, perhaps because they are closer to that early, fragmentary state before any "self" is formed, or perhaps because they are truly not the

masters of their destinies. And although divorce is commonplace enough and often benign—without open rancor between parents—going from *here* to *there* can become a form of
being *nowhere*. The child finds himself *yonder* in a land between father and mother. Because "home" is more than a
place to park the body, because it is necessarily a symbolic
landscape, what can it mean to have two of them? Two homes
inevitably contradict each other, always in small ways, sometimes in big ones. What happens if the words spoken in one
place contradict the words in the other? Where does the child
reside then? And what does it mean for that child's relations to
the symbolic world in general—to language itself as the expression of truth, of all meaning? When Daniel was in the second grade, he invented a place he called the "Half-World." I
think it was in outer space, and all the people who lived in it
were literally cut in two. He wasn't old enough to know why he
had concocted this place, but when he told me about it, I suffered a sharp, terrible pang of recognition. I asked him if those
people could ever be put back together again. He said yes. And
I think he was right. There are ways to sew the Half-World together again, even though it is impossible to change its torn
history. Daniel takes photographs, and some of them are remarkable. Many of them are images of places he has isolated
in ways I would never have imagined. When I look at his shad-
ows cast on sidewalks, his mirror images in windows, the
cracks and ruined lines on his doors of abandoned houses, or
the invasive vines that blur the architecture of a small building, I know that these pictures are threads of himself. He sews
with his camera and in the darkroom. And no matter how
derelict his subjects are, there is radiant order to each and
every picture. They are precisely framed. Every line, every
shadow, is exactly where he wants it to be.

A photograph of a place is not a real place any more than a book is, but we inhabit photographs nevertheless as spectator or as identifying actor. Words are more abstract than images, but images are inevitably born of them. The pictorial drama of reading corresponds to the one of writing. You cannot have one without the other. Reading is active, but writing is more active. Making fiction is making a place for the reader in the text, and this brings up the eternal question of making a book: what to put in and what to leave out. One can argue that there are two kinds of writers in the world: the ones who put it all in and the ones who leave a lot of it out. Sweeping claims can be made about history and these impulses. Inclusion and volume can be understood as a literary idea that began in the eighteenth century, developed in the nineteenth, and lasted through Joyce. (He may have turned literature on its head, but he kept a lot in.) Exclusion, too, can be seen as essential to late modernism, most notably Kafka and Beckett. But these are not useful categories "here." (The reader is "here" with me if he or she has come this far.) There are times when a detailed description of a living room and all its furnishings is annoying, when it gets in the way of reading, and then there are times when it does not. Austen is spare in description. Had she described every object in the Bennet parlor, Paul never would have squeezed in his New Jersey living room among all that clutter, and it seems to me the moral resonance of that book would have been partly lost. On the other hand, I cannot imagine Dickens without his full descriptions of places—the stinking Thames and Mr. Venus's ghastly workshop in *Our Mutual Friend*, for example; but these descriptions, like Sterne's clock in *Tristram Shandy*, are always to a purpose. They accelerate the book. They don't bog it down in pointless novelistic gab. Good books usually say enough about where they happen, but not too much. Enough can be more or less, but it's bad books that treat the reader to his expectations about what a novel or a story or a poem is or *where* it is. There is something comforting about bad books, which is why people read them. Surprise can be a wonderful thing, but, on the whole, people don't want it, any more than most children want their rooms changed. They want what they already know to be confirmed, and they have been richly supplied with these fictional comforts since the late eighteenth century, when the novel became popular with the rise in mass literacy. But the good reader (a quality not at all determined by literary sophistication) wants room to fill in the blanks. Every reader writes the book he or she reads, supplying what isn't there, and that creative invention becomes the book.

For the past four years I've been writing a novel set in my hometown, or rather in a fictional version of Northfield. The town in the book is not the real town, but it resembles it strongly. It has another name, Webster, and although it resembles the real town, its geography is askew. I have taken real places—the Ideal Cafe, the Stuart Hotel, Tiny's Smoke Shop, the Cannon River, and Heath Creek, with their names intact—but I relocated some of these places and gave them new inhabitants. Oddly enough, these changes weren't made for my convenience, and I didn't make them without seeing them in my mind first. The collapsing and shifting of that known landscape came about because it "felt right." The map of fictional Webster isn't identical to the map of Northfield, because the one departs emotionally from the other. Since I began writing the book, I have been back to Northfield several times, every Christmas and once during the summer. When I walk past the Ideal Cafe, where Lily Dahl, the heroine of my novel, works, I don't feel much. I find myself looking closely at it, examining the windows on the second floor, behind which is Lily's imaginary apartment, but it just isn't the place I made for myself in fiction. That place exists in memory, but it isn't "real" memory. My best friend, Heather Clark, and my sisters Liv and Astrid all worked in the Ideal Cafe in the 1970s, when it was in its heyday, and they told me stories about their customers. I stole some of them. I have eaten breakfast and lunch and wolfed down pieces of pie in the Ideal Cafe, and I think I remember pretty well what it looked like when I was in high school, but the imaginary cafe where Lily works has supplanted the one I remember and become more "real" to me. Writing fiction is like remembering what never happened. It mimics memory without being memory. Images appear as textual ground, because this is how the brain works. I am convinced that the processes of memory and invention are linked in the mind. Homer evokes the muse of memory before beginning his tale. And the ancient memory systems developed to enhance recollection were always rooted to places. The speaker wandered through houses in his mind, either real or invented, and located words in various rooms and objects. Cicero articulated an architecture of memory dependent on spaces that were well lit. Murky, cramped little hovels wouldn't do as spatial tools for recollection. Every new draft of a book is the work not only of shrinking and expanding and shrinking again but of finding the book's truth, which means throwing out the lies that tempt me. This work is like dredging up a memory that's been obscured by some comfortable delusion and forcing it "to light," a process that can be excruciating. Fiction exists in the borderland between dream and memory. Like dreams, it distorts for its own purpose, sometimes consciously, sometimes unconsciously, and, like memory, fiction requires an effort of concentration to recall how it *really* was. There have been a few extraordinary books written in the present tense, but by and large it's an awkward form. Fiction usually takes place in the past. Somehow that's its natural place.

Paul often says that it's a strange life, this sitting alone in a room making up people and places, and that in the long run, nobody does it unless he has to. Years ago, he translated a French writer, Joseph Joubert, whose brief but startling journal entries have become part of our ongoing dialogue about art. Joubert wrote: "Those for whom the world is not enough: poets, philosophers and all lovers of books." When I read *Death on the Installment Plan* in my early thirties, the book in which I imagined the hero in my grandparents' house, I loved it so much I was sorry to finish it. I closed the book and shocked myself by thinking, This is better than life. I didn't mean or want to think this, but I'm afraid I did. Certainly this feeling about a book is the one that makes people want to write. I don't know why I feel more alive when I write, but I do. Maybe I imagine that if I scratch hard enough into the paper, I will last. Maybe the world isn't enough, or maybe the distinction between the world and fiction is not so clear. Fiction is made from the stuff of the world, after all, which includes dreams and wishes and fantasies and memory. And it is never really made alone, but from the material between and among us: language. When Mikhail Bakhtin argues that the novel is dialogical—multivoiced, conflicted, in constant dialogue within itself—he is identifying all those jabbering voices every fiction writer hears in his or her head. Writing novels is a solitary act that is also plural, and its many voices are forever placing us somewhere—here or there or yonder. At the same time, writing collapses these spatial categories. Like a heartbeat or a breath, it marks the time of a living consciousness on the page, a consciousness that is present and here, but also absent. The page can resurrect what's lost and what's dead, what's not there anymore and what was never there. Fiction is like the ghost twin of memory that moves through the myriad cities, landscapes, houses, and rooms of the mind.

1995

A Plea for Eros

A FEW YEARS AGO A FRIEND OF MINE GAVE A LECTURE AT
Berkeley on the *femme fatale*, a subject he has been thinking
about for years. When I met him, he was a graduate student
at Columbia University, but now he is a full-fledged philosopher, and when it is finished, his book will be published by
Gallimard in France and Harvard University Press in America. He is Belgian but lives in Paris, a detail significant to the
story, because he comes from another rhetorical tradition—a
French one. When he finished speaking, he took questions, including a hostile one from a woman who demanded to know
what he thought of the Antioch Ruling—a law enacted at Antioch College, which essentially made every stage of a sexual
encounter on campus legal only by verbal consent. My friend
paused, smiled, and replied, "It's wonderful. I love it. Just
think of the erotic possibilities: 'May I touch your right
breast? May I touch your left breast?'" The woman had nothing to say.

This little exchange has lingered in my mind. What inter-
ests me is that he and she were addressing exactly the same
problem, the idea of permission, and yet their perspectives

were so far apart that it was as if they were speaking different languages. The woman expected opposition, and when she didn't get it, she was speechless. Aggressive questions are usually pedagogic—that is, the answer has already been written in the mind of the questioner, who then waits with a reply. It's pretend listening. But by moving the story—in this case, the narrative of potential lovers—onto new ground, the young philosopher tripped up his opponent.

It is safe to assume that the Antioch Ruling wasn't devised to increase sexual pleasure on campus, and yet the new barriers it made, ones that dissect both sexual gestures and the female body (the ruling came about to protect women, not men), have been the stuff of erotic fantasy for ages. When the troubadour pined for his lady, he hoped against hope that he would be granted a special favor—a kiss perhaps. The sonnet itself is a form that takes the body of the beloved apart—her hair, her eyes, her lips, her breasts. The body in pieces is reborn in this legal drama of spoken permission. Eroticism thrives both on borders and on distance. It is a commonplace that sexual pleasure demands thresholds. My philosopher made quick work of demonstrating the excitement of crossing into forbidden territory—the place you need special permission to trespass into. But there is distance here, too, a distance the earnest crusaders who invented the ruling couldn't possibly have foreseen. The articulation of the other's body in words turns it into a map of possible pleasure, effectively distancing that body by transforming it into an erotic object.

Objectification has a bad name in our culture. Cries of "Women are not sexual objects" have been resounding for years. I first ran into this argument in a volume I bought in the ninth grade called *Sisterhood Is Powerful*. I carried that book around with me until it fell apart. Feminism was good for me, as were any number of causes, but as I developed as a thinking person, the truisms and dogmas of every ideology became as worn as that book's cover. Of course women are sexual objects; so are men. Even while I was hugging that book of feminist rhetoric to my chest, I groomed myself carefully, zipped myself into tight jeans, and went after the boy I wanted most, mentally picking apart desirable male bodies like a connoisseur. Erotic pleasure, derived from the most intimate physical contact, thrives on the paradox that only by keeping alive the strangeness of that other person can eroticism last. Every person is keenly aware of the fact that sexual feeling is distinct from affection, even though they often conspire, but this fact runs against the grain of classic feminist arguments.

American feminism has always had a puritanical strain, an imposed blindness to erotic truth. There is a hard, pragmatic aspect to this. It is impolitic to admit that sexual pleasure comes in all shapes and sizes, that women, like men, are often aroused by what seems silly at best and perverse at worst. And because sexual excitement always partakes of the culture itself, finds its images and triggers from the boundaries delineated in a given society, the whole subject is a messy business.

Several years ago I read an article in *The New York Times* about a Chinese version of the Kinsey Report, the results of which suggested that Chinese women as a group experienced *no* sexual pleasure. This struck me as insane, but as I began to ponder the idea, it took on a kind of sense. I visited China in 1986 to find a place still reeling from the Cultural Revolution, a place in which prerevolutionary forms appeared to have been utterly forgotten. Maybe there can't be much erotic life, other than the barest minimum, without an encouraging culture—without movies and books, without ideas about what it's supposed to be. When I was fifteen, I remember watching *Carnal Knowledge* at the Grand movie theater in Northfield, Minnesota, my hometown. Jack Nicholson and Ann-Margret were locked in a mystifying upright embrace and were crashing around the room with their clothes on, or most of them on, banging into walls and making a lot of noise, and I had absolutely no idea what they were doing. It had never occurred to me in my virginal state that people made love *like that*. A friend had to tell me what I was seeing. Most teenagers today are more sophisticated, but only because they've had more exposure. I was thirteen before I stumbled over the word *rape*—in *Gone with the Wind*. I walked downstairs and asked my mother what it meant. She looked at me and said, "I was afraid of that." Then she told me. But even after I knew, I didn't really understand it, and I couldn't imagine it.

My point is this: A part of me has real sympathy for the Chinese couple, both university professors, who married, went to bed with each other faithfully every night, and, after a year, visited a doctor, wondering why no child had come from their union. They thought sleeping *beside* each other was enough. Nobody told them that more elaborate activity was necessary. Surely this is a case of an erotic culture gone with the wind. (In China among the class that could afford to cultivate it, the female body had become a refined aesthetic object. In Xi'an I saw a very old woman with bound feet. She could no longer walk and had to be carried. Those tiny, crippled feet were the gruesome legacy of a lost art. Binding feet made them small enough to fit into a man's mouth.) The famous parental lecture on the birds and the bees, the butt of endless jokes and deemed largely unnecessary in our world, never took place in the lives of the two puzzled professors. *But where were their bodies?* We imagine that proximity would be enough, that *natural* forces would lead the conjugal couple to sexual happiness. But my feeling is that it isn't true, that all of us need a story outside ourselves, a form through which we imagine ourselves as players in the game.

Consider standard erotic images. Garter belts and stockings still have a hold on the paraphernalia of arousal—even though, except for the purpose of titillation, they have mostly vanished from women's wardrobes. Would these garments be sexy if you'd never seen them before? Would they mean anything? But we can't escape the erotic vocabulary of our culture any more than we can escape language itself. There's the rub. Although feminist discourse in America understandably wants to subvert cultural forms that aren't "good" for women, it has never taken on the problem of arousal with much courage. When a culture oppresses women, and all do to one degree or another, it isn't convenient to acknowledge that there are women who like submission in bed or who have fantasies about rape. Masochistic fantasies damage the case for equality, and even when they are seen as the result of a "sick society," the peculiarity of our sexual actions or fantasies is not easily untangled or explained away. The ground from which they spring is simply too muddy. Acts can be controlled, but not desire. Sexual feeling pops up, in spite of our politics.

Desire is always between a subject and an object. People may have loose, roving appetites, but desire must fix on an object even if that object is imaginary, or narcissistic—even if the self is turned into an other. Between two real people, the sticky part is beginning. As my husband says, "Somebody has to make the first move." And this is a delicate matter. It means reading another person's desires. But misreading happens,

too. When I was in my early twenties in graduate school, I
met a brilliant, astoundingly articulate student with whom I
talked and had coffee. I was in love at the time with someone
else, and I was unhappy, but not unhappy enough to end the
relation. This articulate student and I began going to the
movies, sharing Chinese dinners, and talking our heads off. I
gave him poems of mine to read. We talked about books and
more books and became *friends* (as the saying goes). I was
not attracted to him sexually, nor did I glean any sexual interest in me from him. He didn't flirt. He didn't make any moves,
but after several months, our friendship blew up in my face.
It became clear that he had pined and suffered, and that I had
been insensitive. The final insult to him turned on my having
given him a poem to criticize that had as its subject the sexual power of my difficult boyfriend. I felt bad. Perhaps never
in my life have I so misinterpreted a relation with another
person. I have always prided myself on having a nearly un-
canny ability to receive unspoken messages, to sense underly-
ing intentions, even unconscious ones, and here I had
bollixed up the whole story. No doubt we were both to blame.
He was too subtle, and I was distracted—fixated on another
body. Would the Antioch Ruling have helped us? I doubt it. A
person who doesn't reach out for your hand or stroke your
face or come near you for a kiss isn't about to propose these
overtures out loud. He was a person without any coarseness
of mind, much too refined to leap. He thought that dinner
and the movies meant that we were on a "date," that he had
indicated his interest through the form of our evenings. I, on
the other hand, had gone to lots of dinners and movies with
fellow students, both men and women, and it didn't occur to
me that the form signified anything in particular; and yet the
truth was, I should have known. Because he was so discreet,

and because I lacked all sexual feeling for him, I assumed he had none for me.

Nineteenth-century conventions for courtship have been largely disassembled in the latter half of this century, bending the codes out of shape. People marry later. The emphasis on virginity for women has changed. Single women work and are not expected to give up their jobs once they marry. Men have been digesting a set of new rules that are nevertheless colored by the old ones. People still court each other, after all. They are still looking for Romance of one kind or another—short or long—and each one of them is alone out there reading and misreading the intentions of others. The Antioch Ruling was clearly a response to the chaos of courtship—a way of imposing a structure on what seemed to have collapsed—but ambiguity remains, not just in interpretation but even in desire itself. There are people, and we have all met them, who can't make up their minds. There are people who say no when they mean yes, and yes when they mean no. There are people who mean exactly what they say when they say it, and then later wish they had said the opposite. There are people who succumb to sexual pressure out of a misplaced desire to please or even out of pity. To pretend ambiguity doesn't exist in sexual relations is just plain stupid.

And then there are moments of interruption—those walls that block desire. I was absolutely mad about a boy in high school, but there was something about his nose when he kissed me, something about its apparent softness from that angle, that I disliked. To my mind, that nose needed more cartilage. I kept my eyes shut. I know of a woman who fell for a man at a party. She fell hard and fast. They returned to her apartment in an erotic fever, kissing madly, throwing their clothes off, and then she looked across the room and saw his underwear. If I remember correctly, it was some male version of the bikini bottom, and her attraction vanished suddenly, irrevocably. She told the poor man to leave. An explanation was impossible. What was she to say? "I hate your underpants"?

Sexual freedom and eroticism are not identical; in fact, freedom can undermine the erotic, because the no-holds-barred approach is exciting only if you've just knocked down the door. And despite the fact that dinner, a movie, and a kiss at the door have taken a beating in recent years, seduction is inevitably a theater of barriers, a playing and replaying of roles, both conscious and unconscious. Sincerity is not at issue here; most of us play in earnest. Through the language of clothes and gesture and through talk itself, we imagine ourselves as the other person will see us, mirroring our own desire in them, and most of what we do is borrowed from a vocabulary of familiar images. This is not a territory of experience that is easy to dissect legally.

Apparently, there is a new law in Minnesota against staring. It has been duly mocked in newspapers all over the world, but according to my sister, it came about because of the increase in the number of construction sites around Minneapolis, and women were weary of walking past them. Most women have experienced these painful, often humiliating excursions in front of an ogling, jeering crowd of men, and I don't know of anyone who likes them. This event—the construction crew whooping and hooting at a passing woman—is a convention, a thing those guys do in a group and only in a group, to liven up the job, to declare their masculinity to the world *safely*. It's the pseudo-sexual invitation. Not a single one of those men expects the woman to say, "Yes, I'm flattered. Take me, now."

But staring, even staring in this crude from, does not seem

criminal to me. "Officer, he's staring. Arrest him," has a feeble
ring to it. And I say this despite the fact that twice in my life I
found myself the object of what would have to be described
as aggressive staring. For several years, when I was in high
school and then attending college in the same town, a young
man I knew only slightly would appear out of nowhere and
stare. He did not stare casually. He stared wholeheartedly
and with such determination, he made me nervous and uncomfortable, as if he did it to satisfy some deep longing inside him. Without any warning, I would find him stationed
outside the restaurant where I worked or outside the student
union at my college, his eyes fixed on me. They were enormous pale eyes, ringed with black, that made him look as if
he hadn't slept in weeks. "I've been standing here since eight
o'clock this morning," he said to me once at three in the afternoon, "waiting for you." One night after work he followed
me through the streets. I panicked and began to run. He did
not pursue me. The problem was that he acted in ways that
struck me as unaccountable. He would make abrupt changes
in his appearance—suddenly shaving his head, for example.
He walked all the way to my parents' house to deliver a gift,
badly packed in a cardboard box. Filled with dread, I opened
the box, only to find an ugly but innocent green vase. Not long
before I received the vase, this young man's twin brother had
killed himself in a cafe in a nearby town. He had gone there
for breakfast and then, after finishing his meal, took out a gun
and blew his brains out. I am sure I associated the actions of
the twin with the one who survived, am sure that the staring
frightened me because I imagined potential violence lurking
behind those eyes. The looks he gave me were beyond anything I had ever encountered, but I also honestly believe he
meant me no harm. Perhaps in his own way he was in love. I

don't know. But the crux of the story is that I think I brought it on myself without meaning to. Once, when I was in high school, I hugged him.

I worked at a place called the Youth Emergency Service, and the staring boy used to hang out there. I don't know where he lived or how he managed. He didn't go to school. He was sad that day, as he probably was most days, and we talked. I have no recollection of that conversation, but I know that in a fit of compassion I hugged him. I am convinced that the whole staring problem hinged on this hug, and to this day when I think of it I am mortified. Acts cannot be retrieved and, sometimes, they last. This is not a simple story. I often wonder if any story is, if you really look at it, but I carry his face around with me and when I think of him and the former me I feel sorry for both of us.

The other staring man was a student of mine at Queens College. I taught freshman English there and an introductory literature class. My teaching was passionate, occasionally histrionic, but I was a young woman on a mission to educate, and sometimes I did. This student was clearly intelligent, although he had profound and jarring diction problems. His papers were written in a gnarled, convoluted style that was meant to be elevated but was often merely wrong. Eventually, I came to recognize that there were signs of schizophrenia in the writing, but that wasn't until later. I had private sessions with all my students. These meetings were required, and when I met with him, I urged simplicity and hiding his thesaurus forever. The trouble began when he was no longer my student. He would barge into my office unannounced and throw unwanted gifts onto my desk—records, perfume, magazines. He, too, had a penchant for inexplicable transformations, for flannel shirts one day and silky feminine tops the next. On a balmy afternoon in late April, he visited me wearing a fur coat. Another time, I looked up to find him standing in my little graduate-assistant cubicle, his fingers busily unbuttoning his shirt. This story rings with comedy now, but I was aghast. In my best schoolteacher voice, I shouted, "Stop!" He looked terribly hurt and began stamping his foot like a three-year-old, whining my *first* name, as though he couldn't believe I had thwarted him. After that, he would park himself outside the classroom where I taught and stare at me. If I looked a little to the right, I would see him in my peripheral vision. The staring unnerved me, and after several days of it, I was scared. When I crossed the campus, he would follow me—an omnipresent ghost I couldn't shake. Talking to him did no good. Yelling at him did no good. I went to the college police. They were indifferent to my alarm. No, more than that, they were contemptuous. I had no recourse. In time, the student gave up, and my ghost disappeared, never to bother me again. The question is, What does this story exemplify? Would it be called "sexual harassment" now, because of the shirt episode? Was it stalking? What he actually *did* to me was innocuous. The fear came from the fact that what he did was unpredictable. He did not play by the rules, and once those rules had been broken, I imagined that anything was possible.

Neither of these staring experiences was erotic for me, but they may have been for the two young men who did the staring. Who I was for either of them remains a mystery to me, a blank filled with my own dread. They have lasted inside me as human signs of the mysteries of passion, of emotional disturbance and tumult, and despite the unpleasantness they caused me, I am not without compassion for both of them. I have stared myself. Looking hard is the first sign of eros, and once, when I was fourteen, I found myself staring very hard at a house. I had fallen in love with a boy who was fifteen. He cared nothing for me and was involved with a girl who had what I didn't have: breasts. She fascinated me almost as much as he did, because, after all, she was his beloved, and I studied her carefully for clues to her success. One Saturday in the fall, I walked to his house, stood outside on the sidewalk, and stared at it for a long time. I'm not sure why I did this. Perhaps I hoped he would walk out the door, or maybe I thought I might gain the courage to ring the bell. I remember that the house looked deserted. Probably no one was home. It was a corner house on a beautiful street in Northfield, lined with elms. The elms are all dead now, but I remember the street with trees. That house, which once was his house, is still suffused with the memory of my terrible ache for him, a longing I found almost unbearable and which was never requited. Years later, when I was grown (much taller than he ever grew) and I saw him in a local bar, he remembered my "crush" and said he regretted not acting on it. As silly as it sounds, this confession of his gave me real satisfaction, but the fact is he didn't want the fourteen-year-old I had been but the twenty-two-year-old I had become—another person altogether.

Ogling should be legal. Looking is part of love, but what you see when you look is anybody's guess. Why that skinny ninth-grade boy with glasses sent me into paroxysms of longing I couldn't tell you, but he did. Feelings are crude. The ache of love feels remarkably like the ache of grief or guilt. Emotional pain isn't distinguishable by feeling, only by language. We give a name to the misery, not because we recognize the feeling but because we know its context. Sometimes we feel bad and don't know why or don't remember why. Mercifully, love is sometimes equal and two people, undisturbed by the wrong underwear or the wrong nose, find each other inside this mystery of attraction and are happy. But why?

Contentment in love usually goes unquestioned. Still, I don't think enduring love is rational any more than momentary flings. I have been married to the same man for fifteen years, and I can't explain why he still attracts me as an erotic object. He does, but why? Shouldn't it all be worn out by now? It is *not* because we are so close or know each other so well. That solidifies our friendship, not our attraction. The attraction remains because there's something about him that I can't reach, something strange and estranging. I like seeing him from a distance. I know that. I like to see him in a room full of people when he looks like a stranger, and then to remember that I do know him and that I will be going home with him. But why he sometimes strikes me as a magical being, a person unlike others, I can't tell you. He has many good features, but so do other men who leave me cold as a stone. Have I given him this quality because it is efficient for me, or is it actually in him, some piece of him that I will never conquer and never know? It must be both. It must be between us—an enchanted space that is wholly unreasonable and, at least in part, imaginary. There is still a fence for me to cross and, on the other side of it, a secret.

Love affairs and marriages stand or fall on this secret. Familiarity and the pedestrian realities of everyday life are the enemies of eros. Emma Bovary watches her husband eat and is disgusted. She studies maps of Paris and hopes for something grander, more passionate, unfamiliar. A friend of mine told me about evenings out with her husband, during which they seduce each other all over again and she can't wait to get home and jump on his beautiful body; but if on the way into the house he pauses to straighten the lids on the garbage cans, the spell is broken. She told him, and he now resists this urge. These interruptions disturb the stories we tell ourselves, the ready-made narratives that we have made our own. A combination of biology, personal history, and a cultural miasma of ideas creates attraction. The fantasy lover is always hovering above or behind or in front of the real lover, and you need both of them. The problem is that the alliance of these two is unpredictable. Eros, after all, was a mischievous little imp with arrows, a fellow of surprises who delighted in striking those who expected it least. Like his fairy reincarnation, Puck in *A Midsummer Night's Dream*, he turns the world upside down. Hermia prefers Lysander to Demetrius for no good reason. Shakespeare's young men Demetrius and Lysander, as has often been pointed out, are as alike and interchangeable as two pears. When Theseus points out to Hermia that Demetrius is just as good as Lysander, he isn't lying. It's just that Demetrius is not the one she likes. After much confusion and silliness, the lovers are set right by magic. Demetrius is never disenchanted. The flower juice remains in his eyes and he marries Helena under its influence, the point being that when we fall in love we've all got fairy juice in our eyes, and not one of us gives a jot about the sane advice of parents or friends or governments.

And that's why legislating desire is unwieldy. A child rushes over and kisses another child in a New York City school, and he's nabbed by the authorities for "sexual harassment." Maybe it was an aggressive act, a sudden lack of control that needed the teacher's attention. Maybe the kissed child was unhappy or scared. And maybe, contrary to the myth of childish innocence, it was *sexual*, a burst of strange, wild feeling. I don't know. But people, children and adults, do bump up against each other. Everywhere, all the time, there are scuffles of desire. We have laws against molestation and rape. Using power and position to extract sexual favors from an unwilling employee is ugly and shouldn't be legal. But on the other side of these crimes is a blurry terrain, a borderland of dreams and wishes. And it isn't a landscape of sunshine only. It is a place streaked with the clouds of sadism and masochism, where peculiar objects and garments are strewn here and there, and where its inhabitants weep as often as they sigh with pleasure. And it is nothing less than amazing that we should have to be reminded of this. All around us, popular singers are crooning out their passion and bitterness on the radio. Billboards, advertisements, and television shows are playing to our erotic weaknesses twenty-four hours a day. But at the same time, there is a kind of spotty cultural amnesia in particular circles, a blockheaded impulse to crush complexity and truth in the name of right-thinking.

Once when I was attending a panel discussion on the fate or the state of "the novel" at the 92nd Street Y, because my husband had been roped into moderating this discussion, I listened to a novelist, an intelligent and good writer, berate Kafka for his depictions of women. They were bad, she said, wrongheaded. But in Kafka's world of dreams and claustrophobia, a world of irreducible images so powerful that they shake me every time I remember them, what does it mean to second-guess its genius, to edit out the women who lift their skirts for the wandering K.? When I read Kafka, I am not that housemaid who presents herself to the tormented hero anyway. I am the hero, the one who takes the pleasure offered, as we all do when we sleep.

This is my call for eros, a plea that we not forget ambiguity and mystery, that in matters of the heart we acknowledge an abiding uncertainty. I honestly think that when we are possessed by erotic magic we don't feel like censoring Kafka or much else, because we are living a story of exciting thresholds and irrational feeling. We are living in a secret place we make between us, a place where the real and unreal commingle. That's where the young philosopher took the woman with the belligerent question. He brought her into a realm of the imagination and of memory, where lovers are alone speaking to each other, saying yes or no or "perhaps tomorrow," where they play at who they are, inventing and reinventing themselves as subjects and objects; and when the woman with the question found herself there, she was silent. Maybe, just maybe, she was remembering a passionate story of her own.

1996

Gatsby's *Glasses*

I FIRST READ *THE GREAT GATSBY* WHEN I WAS SIXTEEN YEARS old, a high school student in Northfield, Minnesota. I read it again when I was twenty-three and living in New York City, and now again at the advanced age of forty-two. I have carried the book's magic around with me ever since that first reading, and its memory is distinct in my mind, because unlike many books that return to me chiefly as a series of images, *The Great Gatsby* has also left its trace in my ear—as enchanted music, whispering, laughter, and as the voice of storytelling itself.

The book begins with the narrator's memory of something his father told him years before: "Whenever you feel like criticizing anyone, remember that all the people in this world haven't had the advantages that you've had." As an adage for life, the quotation is anticlimactic—restrained words I imagine being uttered by a restrained man, perhaps over the top of his newspaper, and yet without this watered-down American version of noblesse oblige, there could be no story of Gatsby. The father's words are the story's seed, its origin. The man who we come to know as Nick Carraway tells us that his father "meant a great deal more" than what the words denote, and I believe him. Hidden in the comment is a way of living and an entire moral world. Its resonance is double: first, we know that the narrator's words are bound to his father's words, that he comes from somewhere he can identify, and that he has not severed that connection; and second, we know that these paternal words have shaped him into who he is, a man "inclined to reserve all judgements"—in short, the ideal narrator, a man who doesn't leap into the action but stays on the sidelines. Nick is not an actor but a voyeur, and in every art, including the art of fiction, there's always somebody watching.

Taking little more than his father's advice, the young man goes east. The American story has changed direction: the frontier is flip-flopped from west to east, but the urge to leave home and seek your fortune is as old as fairy tales. Fitzgerald's Middle West was not the same as mine. I did not come from the stolid advantages of Summit Avenue in St. Paul. I remember those large, beautiful houses on that street as beacons of wealth and privilege to which I had no access. I grew up in the open spaces of southern Minnesota in one of the "lost Swede towns" Fitzgerald mentions late in the book, only we were mostly Norwegians, not Swedes. It was to my hometown that Fitzgerald sent Gatsby to college for two weeks. The unnamed town is Northfield. The named college is St. Olaf, where my father taught for thirty years and where I was a student for four. Gatsby's ghost may have haunted me, because even in high school I knew that promise lay in the East, particularly in New York City, and ever so vaguely, I began to dream of what I had never seen and where I had never been.

Nick Carraway hops a train and finds himself in the bond trade and living next door to Gatsby's huge mansion: a house built of wishes. All wishes, however wrongheaded, however great or noble or ephemeral, must have an object, and that object is usually more ideal than real. The nature of Gatsby's wish is fully articulated in the book. Gatsby is *great*, because his dream is all-consuming and every bit of his strength and breath is in it. He is a creature of will, and the beauty of his will overreaches the tawdriness of his real object: Daisy. But the secret of the story is that there is no *great Gatsby* without Nick Carraway, only Gatsby, because Nick is the only one who is able to see the greatness of Gatsby's wish.

Reading the book again, I was struck by the strangeness of a single sentence that seemed to glitter like a golden key to the story. It occurs when a dazed Gatsby finds his wish granted and he is showing Daisy around the West Egg mansion. Nick is, as always, the third wheel. "I tried to go then," he says, "but they wouldn't hear of it; perhaps my presence made them feel more satisfactorily alone." The question is: In what way are two people more *satisfactorily* alone when somebody else is present? What on earth does this mean? I have always felt that there is a triangular quality to every love affair. There are two lovers and a third element—the idea of being in love itself. I wonder if it is possible to fall in love without this third presence, an imaginary witness to love as a thing of wonder, cast in the glow of our deepest stories about ourselves. It is as if Nick's eyes satisfy this third element, as if he embodies for the lovers the essential self-consciousness of love—a third-person account. When I read Charles Scribner III's introduction to my paperback edition, I was not at all surprised that an early draft of the novel was written by Fitzgerald in the third person. Lowering the narration into the voice of a character inside the story allows the writer to inhabit more fully the interstices of narrative itself.

The role of the onlooker is given quasi-supernatural status in the book in the form of the bespectacled eyes of T. J. Eckleburg, and it is to this faded billboard of an oculist in Queens that the grieving Wilson addresses his prayer: "You can't hide from God." When his friend tells him, "That's an advertisement," Wilson doesn't answer. The man needs an omniscient third person, and he finds it in Eckleburg, with his huge staring eyes. This speech occurs when Nick is not present, and yet the quality of the narration does not change. It is *as if* he were present. Nick's stand-in is a neighbor of Wilson's, Michaelis, who has presumably reported the scene to the narrator, but the reader isn't told this directly. Together, Michaelis and Nick Carraway form a complementary narration that finds transcendence in the image of Eckleburg's all-seeing, all-knowing eyes, a figure very like the third-person narrator of nineteenth-century novels who looks down on his creatures and their follies.

There is only one other noticeable pair of spectacles in the novel, those worn by "the owl-eyed man." One of Gatsby's hundreds of anonymous guests, he is first seen in the "Gothic library," a drunken fellow muttering excitedly that the books "are absolutely real." He had expected cardboard, he tells Nick and Jordan, and cannot get over his astonishment at the *reality* of these volumes. The owl-eyed man returns near the end of the book as Gatsby's only mourner besides the dead man's father and Nick. Like the image of Eckleburg, the owl-eyed man is both thoroughly mysterious and thoroughly banal. He tells Nick and Jordan that he's been drunk for a week and that he thought the books might help "sober" him up. Nameless, the man is associated exclusively with the library and his large glasses. Nick does not ask the owl-eyed man to attend the funeral. He has kept the day and place a secret to avoid gawkers and the press, but, out of nowhere, the man makes his appearance in the rain, and during that time he removes his glasses twice. The second time, he wipes them, "outside and in." I can see him doing it. For me the gesture is intimate, and although no handkerchief is mentioned, I see a white handkerchief, too, moving over the rain-spattered lenses. The cleaning of the glasses is ordinary and magical. The strange man is a second, specifically literary incarnation of Eckleburg, a witness to the problem of what's real and what isn't, a problem that is turned inside out through the idea of seeing through *special glasses*—the glasses of fiction.

The Great Gatsby is an oddly immaterial novel. In it there are only two characters with bodies that mean anything, bodies of vigor and appetite: Tom Buchanan and his mistress, Myrtle Wilson, whose alliance causes the book's tragedy. The rest of them, Gatsby, the hordes of guests, Jordan, and, above all, Daisy, seem to be curiously unanchored to the ground. They are pastel beings, beings of light and sound—creatures of the imagination. At Gatsby's parties, "men and girls" come and go "like moths," accompanied by an orchestra as if they were characters in a play or a movie. When Nick first sees Daisy and Jordan in East Egg, the girls are reclining on a huge sofa. "They were both in white, and their dresses were rippling and fluttering as if they had just been blown back in after a short flight around the room." They are as weightless as dollar bills, or maybe hundred-dollar bills, blown up in a wind before they settle again to the ground, and whether or not Fitzgerald intended this lightness as another image of money in his novel, money is the source of the charm that envelops the ethereal creatures. Daisy's music is her own "thrilling" voice, and it sounds, as Gatsby says, "like money." But Nick is the one who elaborates on its timbre. In it he hears the jingle of coins and the rain of gold in fairy tales.

It may be that New York and its environs is the best place in the world to feel this particular bewitchment that all the pieties about honest poverty cannot disperse. Fitzgerald is right. Money in the Midwest may be respectable and it may even be considerable, but it is nothing like New York money. There was no money where I grew up, no "real" money, that is. The turkey farmers did well, and the dentists in town had a certain affluent shine to them, but, on the whole, status was measured in increments—a new *economy* car, unused skates, an automatic garage door opener—and there was a feeling that it was wrong to have much more money than anybody else, and downright sinful to flaunt it if you had it. When I arrived in New York, the money I saw flabbergasted me. It sashayed on Fifth Avenue and giggled in galleries and generally showed itself off with such unabashed glee that it was impossible not to admire it or envy it, at least a little. And what I saw during my travels through the city in the early 1980s was no different from what Nick saw. Money casts a glow over things, a glow all the more powerful to people who haven't got it. No matter how clean or morally upright, poverty has cracks and corners of ugliness that nothing but money can close, and I remember the sense of relief and pleasure that would come over me when I sat in a good restaurant with white tablecloths and shining silver and flowers and I knew that my date was a person who could afford to pay. And it happened during my lonely, impoverished student days that a man would lean across the table and invite me to an island or to another country or to a seaside resort, to an East Egg or a West Egg, and the truth was that the smell of money would waft over me, its scent like a torpor-inducing drug, and had there been no Middle West, no Northfield, Minnesota, no home with its strident Lutheran sanctions, no invisible parental eyes always watching me—in short: had I been somebody else—I might have been blown off to an Egg in a gust of wind and floated across the beach and out into the Sound to the strains of some foolish but melodic accompaniment.

Gravity is personal history. That is why Nick tells the reader about his family right away. The Carraways have been "prominent well-to-do people for three generations," three generations founded on the rock of a *hardware* business, a business that trades in real *things*. In the East, Nick trades not in things, as his father does, but in paper, bonds that will generate more paper. Money that makes money. And money has built Gatsby's castle, a place as unreal as a theater set erected from bills or bonds or "cardboard," as the owl-eyed man suggests. It is a blur of excess and anonymity as vague as Gatsby's rumored past—a past we learn in bits and pieces but which is never whole, for he is a man interrupted, a man who has broken from his old life and his parents to become not somebody else so much as "Nobody," a brilliant cipher. "Mr. Nobody from Nowhere" is Tom Buchanan's contemptuous expression. Gatsby's connections to others are tenuous or fabricated. He misrepresents himself to Daisy when he first meets her in Louisville, by implying that he comes from her world. Again the image of wind appears in Fitzgerald's prose: "As a matter of fact, he had no comfortable family standing behind him, and he was liable at the whim of an impersonal government to be blown anywhere about the world."

But in this ephemeral weightlessness of Gatsby's there is beauty, real beauty, and on this the whole story turns. The man's monstrous accumulation of *things* is nothing if not vulgar, a grotesque display as pitiful as it is absurd. But what

Nick understands, as nobody else does, is that this mountain of things is the vehicle of a man's passion, and as objects they are nearly drained of material reality. The afternoon when Gatsby takes Daisy through his house, we are told that he "stares at his possessions in a dazed way, as though in her actual and astounding presence, none of it was any longer real." His nerves running high, the owner of the property begins pulling shirts from his closet, one gauzy, gorgeous article after another, "in coral and apple-green and lavender and faint orange, with monograms of Indian blue," piling them high before Nick and his beloved. Then Daisy bends her lovely head and weeps into the shirts: "It makes me sad because I've never seen such—such beautiful shirts before." I marveled again at the power of this passage, which is at once tender and ridiculous. But Fitzgerald lets neither feeling get the upper hand. Daisy pours out the grief of her young love for Gatsby into a heap of his splendid shirts without understanding her own feelings. But she recovers quickly. Sometime later the same afternoon, she stares out the window at pink clouds in a western sky and says to Gatsby, "I'd just like to get one of those pink clouds and put you in it and push you around." The shirts, the clouds, the dream are colored like a fading rainbow. Gatsby stands at the edge of his lawn and watches the green light across the water from Daisy's house. The last suit Nick sees him wearing is pink. If your feet are rooted to the ground, you can't be blown willy-nilly, but you can't fly up to those rosy clouds either. It's as simple as that.

Things and nothings. Bodies and nobodies. The ground and the air. The tangible and the intangible. The novel moves restlessly between these dichotomies. Surely Fitzgerald was right when he said that *The Great Gatsby* was "a new thinking out of the idea of illusion." Illusion is generally coupled with its opposite, reality, but where is the real? Is reality found in the tangible and illusion in the intangible? Besides the nuts and bolts of hardware out west, there is *ground* in the novel, the soil of ashes in West Egg, the ground that Eckleburg unblinkingly surveys, but it is here that Fitzgerald lavishes a prose that could have been taken straight from Dickens, a prose of fantasy, not realism.

> This is the valley of ashes—a fantastic farm where ashes grow like wheat into ridges and hills and grotesque gardens; where ashes take the forms of houses and chimneys and rising smoke, and finally, with a transcendent effort, of men who move dimly and already crumbling through the powdery air.

With its crumbling men, the valley of ashes plainly evokes that other biblical valley of death, and this miserable stretch of land borders the road where Myrtle Wilson will die under the wheels of the car driven by Daisy. But like the pink clouds, it lacks solidity and dissolves. The difference between the vision of Gatsby's mansion and this earth is that money does not disguise mortality here. The gaping cracks of poverty are fully visible.

Nevertheless, among the residents of this ashen valley is Myrtle Wilson, the only person in the novel to whom Fitzgerald assigns "vitality." The word is used three times in reference to Mrs. Wilson, Tom Buchanan's working-class mistress: ". . . there was an immediately perceptible *vitality* about her as if the nerves of her body were continually smouldering." As Nick passes Wilson's gas station in a car, he sees her "at the garage pump with panting *vitality*." And in death: "The mouth was wide open and ripped at the corners, as though she had choked a little in giving up the tremendous *vitality* she had stored so long." It is this vivid life, not her character, that makes Myrtle Wilson's death tragic. A silly and coarse woman, she is nevertheless more sympathetic than her lover, Tom, who is worse: stupid and violent. Between them, however, there exists a real sexual energy that isn't found elsewhere in the novel. The narrator's attraction to Jordan is tepid at best, and Gatsby's fantasies about Daisy seem curiously unerotic. The slender girl has no body to speak of. She seems to be made of her beautiful clothes and her beautiful voice. It is hard to imagine Gatsby actually having sex with Daisy. It's like trying to imagine a man taking a butterfly. And although her marriage to Tom has produced a daughter, as a mother Daisy communicates detachment. She coos endearments at the child, Pammy, and then dismisses her. Only once in the novel is the reader reminded of Daisy as a creature of flesh and blood, and, significantly, it is through a finger her husband has bruised. Daisy looks down at the little finger "with an awed expression." "You didn't mean to," she says to Tom, "but you *did* do it." The passage is not only a premonition of Tom's brutality that erupts horribly in New York when he breaks Myrtle's nose or of Myrtle's bruised and opened body on the road. Daisy's awe expresses her remote relation to her own body and to mortality itself, which her money will successfully hide, not forever, of course, but for now.

What Tom and Myrtle have that Jay and Daisy don't is a *personal* relation, with its attendant physicality and mess. That is why, after admitting to Nick that Daisy may have once loved Tom "for a minute," Gatsby comforts himself by saying, "In any case, it was only personal." What Gatsby has been chasing all these years is neither *personal* nor *physical*. Its transcendence may have been lodged in the person of Daisy, but it is not limited to her. Her very shallowness makes Gatsby's dream possible. But Myrtle Wilson is not a simple incarnation of the flesh and its weaknesses. She harbors dreams as well. As it does for Gatsby, her intangible wish finds form in an object. In her drawer at home, wrapped in tissue paper, Mr. Wilson finds the expensive dog leash Tom once bought for her to go with the dog he also bought. The dog didn't come home. The useless, beautiful thing is a sign of absence, a string of absences, in fact—the dog, the lover, and the emptiness of desire itself. Just as the green light shining from Daisy's house may be counted among Gatsby's "enchanted objects," one he loses when Daisy actually enters his life again, the dog leash possesses a kind of magic. It is the tissue paper that makes me want to cry, that sends this frivolous possession into another register altogether, that imbues the silver-and-leather dog leash with the quality of true pathos.

The tangible and the intangible collide to cast a spell. But can a person or thing ever be stripped naked? Can we ever discover reality hiding under the meanings we give to people and things? I don't think so. And I don't think Fitzgerald thought so either. His book meditates on the necessity of fiction, not only as lies but as truths. The play between the material and the immaterial in *The Great Gatsby* is riddled, not simple. The fairy tale contains the valley of ashes as well as the castle by the sea, the heavy weight of the corpse and the pretty bodies blown in the wind. And which one is more real than the other? Is death more true than life? Are not dreams as much a part of living as waking life is? The book goes to the heart of the problem of fiction itself by insisting that fiction is necessary to life—not only as books but as dreams, dreams that frame the world and give it meaning. Nick imagines Gatsby at the pool just before Wilson kills him. The man has understood that there will be no message from Daisy, that the great idea is dead.

> He must have looked up at an unfamiliar sky through frightening leaves and shivered as he found what a grotesque thing a rose is and how raw the sunlight was upon the scarcely created grass. A new world, material without being real, where poor ghosts, breathing dreams like air, drifted fortuitously about . . . like that ashen, fantastic figure gliding toward him through the amorphous trees.

This passage tells of dramatic change, but it is not a change from illusion to reality, from enchanted nature to real nature. This world may be new, but there are ghosts here, and they are fantastic. It is now a world made of matter, but that matter is no more real than the magic lights and music of the summer parties that went before it.

One can argue that nearly every word of dialogue uttered in the novel, every exchange, and every event is ordinary. Tom Buchanan and the poor Wilsons are glaringly limited and unattractive. Gatsby's business partner, Wolfsheim, is clever and dishonest without the grandeur of being satanic. Daisy's charm is not revealed in anything she says. Gatsby converses in a stiff and clichéd manner that sets Nick back on his heels. Jordan is a cheat. These characters do not elevate themselves above the crowd. They are not remarkable people, and yet to read this novel is to feel as if you have taken a walk in a fairy wood, as if while you are reading you glimpse the sublime.

The magic is in the book's narration, in its shades of sunlight and darkness, its allusions to folk tales, to music, songs, to dusty dance slippers and bright voices. Better than any other writer I know, Fitzgerald captures the tipsy aura of parties, that slight glazing of the mind that dawns after two glasses of champagne. The ordinary world trembles with *adjectival* enchantment here—Fitzgerald's prose is dense with surprising adjectives. Although some of his characters are glib, the narrator is not. The sorcery that infuses the book cannot be explained as the golden effect of money, although that is part of it, or even by youth. They are mostly very young, these people, and life still holds an unwrapped newness for them. Nick Carraway's voice carries a deeper understanding of enchantment, which at once grounds and elevates the narration. It returns us to the beginning. The father's words render up a world in which every human being, no matter how flawed, is granted an essential dignity. Remember, every person is a product of his own history, one that is not necessarily like yours. He or she has come out of a particular story, and to judge that man or woman is not fair unless you know the story. The advice is a call to empathy, the ultimate act of the imagination, and the true ground of all fiction. All characters are born of this effort to be another person. And its success is rooted in the grounded self. The "carelessness" of Tom and Daisy manifests itself in flightiness. Unballasted, they flit from one place to another, and their wealth only facilitates their disconnectedness. Yet we trust Nick, this man who speaks to us, and we believe him when he says, "I am one of the few honest people that I have ever known." And we trust his *imaginings*, because the imaginary is crucial to his tale. He did not witness Gatsby's murder. He cannot be Gatsby, but he says, "He must have . . ." Nick Carraway's voice bears the conviction of his empathy.

Fitzgerald did not give part of Nick's story to Michaelis because it was convenient. By seamlessly transferring Nick's vision into Wilson's Greek neighbor, Fitzgerald lifts the narration out of the "merely personal." Nick sees beyond himself, and this second sight is reinforced by the eyes of Eckleburg and the owl eyes of the man in the library. Nick sees vicariously what Michaelis and another man actually witness: Myrtle's dead body, the body Daisy will not see and cannot face. It is more than enough. The men undo Mrs. Wilson's shirt "still wet with perspiration" and see "that her left breast was hanging loose like a flap, and there was no need to listen to the heart below." Later, Nick tells Gatsby, "She was ripped open." He did not have to be there to see. For a moment, with Nick, the reader stares into the heart of being, and it has stopped. I see what I did not see. I experience that which is outside my own experience. This is the magic of reading novels. This is the working out of the problem of illusion. I take a book off the shelf. I open it up and begin to read, and what I discover in its pages is real.

1997

Franklin Pangborn: An Apologia

I DON'T KNOW WHEN MR. FRANKLIN PANGBORN FIRST CAME TO my attention. A man of the screen's margins, his legacy comes of repetitions. He pops up in one movie here, in another there. He rules a moment or a full-fledged scene, never an entire film. It was only after I had seen many American films of the thirties and forties that his name came to signify the pompous underling for whom I have come to feel affection. I like the reliability of his character, and I like his name. It combines the elevated connotations of *Franklin*, as in Ben and Roosevelt, with the pathos of *pang*, and the fact that this *pang* is married to *born* delights me with its Dickensian aptness.

With certain modulations, Pangborn always played the same man. Before he uttered a word, his character was in place. The quintessential tight-ass, he held himself in constant check. His posture erect to the point of distortion: back swayed, butt out, chin raised a quarter of an inch, his gestures colored by a shade of snooty effeminacy, he is the man who, if he remains on the screen long enough, will be brought down. His is a ridiculous life, a life of rules maintained at all costs, of self-inflated dignity, of the fully buttoned suit, of obsessive cleanliness, of correctness. When he speaks, his voice swells with enunciations that are decidedly un-American. In truth, his tone bears a suspicious resemblance to that other English, sometimes known as the King's. For Americans, this accent connotes either genuine grandness or pretension. Pangborn has the voice of the small-time snob.

But why do I find Franklin Pangborn endearing? Why do I get pleasure from this altogether persnickety being who returns in one movie after another? It is partly because he is always ineffectual. In a position of real power the same character turns loathsome, but Pangborn appears time and again as the "manager" of something—store, hotel, apartment building—whose directives are subverted by the bedlam that takes place around him. And yet his desire to keep order, to maintain boundaries, to ignore the madness of others has a

noble as well as pathetic dimension. Guided by decorum, the stiff man carries on, often ruffled but rarely defeated. He is the very image of threatened civility.

When I was growing up, my Norwegian mother had ideas about form, attachments to the signs of bourgeois life, which did not always match my American father's more democratic ideals. Not long ago my mother told me that, at least in Norway, one never put out candles for a dinner without having lit the wicks. The candles should not be stumps. They may be new, but the wicks must be blackened before guests arrive at the house. I asked my mother why. "I have no idea," she said, and laughed. "That's just the way it was." I now ignite my wicks before my guests arrive for a dinner party. Surely this shows a Pangbornian aspect to my personality, a will to form wholly unrelated to reason. Of course my father had no objection to blackened wicks. It is possible that he never even noticed this sign of good manners throughout his now forty-four-year marriage to my mother. Wicks fell under her domain—a domestic and feminine one.

My parents differed on the issue of fences, however, a deeper dispute that has further Pangbornian significance. My mother yearned for a fence around our property in Minnesota. For her it had nostalgic resonance, the comfort of enclosure, as well as aesthetic value. As a European, fences seemed natural to her. My father grew up as a farm boy on the prairie. He remembers barn raisings, quilting bees, and square dances. Fences reined in cows, but the idea of delineating one's property smacked of the unneighborly. Pangborn is a character defined by fences, formal divisions that articulate boundaries, difference, hierarchies. In terms of broad American mythology, these fences have a feminine quality. Franklin Pangborn's character stands in stubborn opposition to a freewheeling, democratic, masculine ideal as seen through the lens of American movies in the nineteen thirties and forties.

In an early, brief appearance in Preston Sturges's *The Palm Beach Story,* Pangborn, the manager of an apartment building on Park Avenue, leads potential tenants to the apartment of a couple played by Claudette Colbert and Joel McCrea who, having fallen on hard times, have not paid the rent. Elegant in a dark, close-fitting suit, a spotless white handkerchief protruding from his breast pocket, Pangborn serves as a foil to the near-deaf Weenie King, a western millionaire in a shabby light-colored overcoat and cowboy hat, who is accompanied by his overdressed wife. As unrefined as he is loaded, the King bangs on the walls of the corridor with his cane and shouts non sequiturs while Pangborn works hard to maintain his dignity in the face of these vulgar high jinks. A Hollywood fantasy of the American West, the Weenie King doesn't give a damn about form, grammar, deportment, or fences of any kind. Pangborn answers most of the King's initial questions with the refrain "of course," interrupted by a telltale clearing of his throat, a tic that recurs in the Pangborn persona. It is as if the sum of his disapproval has lodged itself as a bit of phlegm in his throat. The Weenie King's wife notices that the apartment is dirty. The manager acknowledges this and apologizes. But the King yells that he likes dirt, that it's as natural as (among other things) "disease" and "cyclones." Sturges knows dirt is the bottom line here. Pangborn is nothing if not immaculate.

Some time after I became an adult I began to clean. I have become a zealous cleaner, a scrubber of floors, a bleacher, a general enemy of dirt and dust and stains. It is probably unnecessary to say that my mother has cleaned fervently all her life. My husband, who occasionally discovers me in these endeavors—down on my hands and knees in the recesses of some closet—has been known to cry, "Stop!" He takes the long view of order and cleanliness. Why hang up your jacket if you are going to wear it in an hour when you go out? Why empty the ashtray when you can fit in one last cigar butt? Why indeed? I organize and I clean, because I love to see the lines of every object around me clearly delineated, because in my domestic life I fight blur, ambiguity, cyclones, and decay (if not disease). It is a classically feminine position, which is not to say that there aren't scores of men who find themselves in it. I don't know if Pangborn is ever seen actually cleaning in a film, but it is not necessary to see him at it. His character is spotless and obsessive, a figure of perfect order. In terms of American mythology, he is a traitor to his sex, an anti-cowboy who has joined the girls. The fun consists in rumpling him, making him sweat and stumble and get dirty.

Sturges, ever alert to the class bias of Americans who nevertheless revel in the excesses of money, makes the western Weenie King the movie's fairy godfather. The King peels off bills from a bankroll twice the size of his fist and hands them out to the lady of the apartment, whom he discovers hiding in the shower. Pangborn is left in the large living room of the upper-crusty flat, exhausted and appalled at the rigors he is forced to endure in the course of a day's work, rigors that have left him a little crumpled.

Without western populism and its Weenie Kings, the Franklin Pangborn character could not have the same force. Uppity, pinched, urban, and sissified, he is a figure of prairie prejudices, whose elevated diction and manners are a target of ridicule. In *My Man Godfrey* we see him for only a few seconds, but those seconds are important. As Depression wish fulfillment, this film remains among the best. Typically, Pangborn plays a fellow attempting to run things in a climate of chaos. One guesses that he is the chairman of the misguided charity committee, which has organized a scavenger hunt for the very rich. Among the "objects" the players have been asked to bring in is "a forgotten man." Carole Lombard discovers William Powell (Godfrey) in a dump by the river, and after considerable back-and-forth, the daffy but good-hearted creature played by Lombard brings the unshaven, ragged Godfrey into a glittering party of people in gowns and tails. Pangborn tests the forgotten man's authenticity by seeking permission to feel Godfrey's whiskers. (Another player has tried to cheat with an imposter.) Pangborn does this with a bow of his head, the words "May I?" and a clearing of the wonderful throat. But it is his gesture that wins my heart. He lifts his fingers and, with a flourish not seen since the eighteenth-century French court, waves a hand in the direction of the beard and declares it real. It is a beautiful moment. In that hand we see both the rigors of politeness, which forbid intimate contact with another's body, and the distaste for a body that is unwashed, unperfumed, and generally unacceptable. After being declared the genuine article, a truly forgotten man, Godfrey dubs the company around him "a bunch of nitwits," is hired by Lombard as a butler, and the story begins.

I have now lived in New York for twenty years and have wound up from time to time among the nitwits. Although I have never subscribed to the bias of my hometown—that the rich are worse than other people—it is true that vast sums of money have a tendency to look ridiculous from the outside, that the spectacle of spending and playing has a tawdry appearance that turns the stomach of the born-and-bred midwesterner. For a sight of pure silliness and smug self-congratulation, little can compete with the charity ball. They knew this in Hollywood and used it. When my grandparents' farm was going to ruin in Minnesota, there were city slickers in New York who had managed to hold on to their dough. *My Man Godfrey* played for audiences in the sticks, too, audiences that feasted on the opulence of the grand New York house while they laughed at the absurdities of those who lived in it. Godfrey is the frog prince of an American fairy tale, a man whose experience of poverty transforms him. Pangborn, on the other hand, defies enchantment. The static being of bureaucratic management, he will never be transformed.

This stasis finds its best expression in W. C. Fields's *The Bank Dick*. Pangborn plays the bank examiner, J. Pinkerton Snoopington. In tight black suit, bowler hat, and pince-nez, he is the picture of a stick-in-the-mud. Pangborn's fate is to be nearly done in by Fields—Egbert Sousé. Fields's hatred of banks and bankers is well known. And although his aesthetic is anarchic, not agrarian-populist, misanthropic, not humanist, his spleen against bankers must have struck a deep chord among audiences in 1940. It is worth remembering that torturing a bank examiner had greater fantasy value at that time than it does now.

W. C. Fields was not a great champion of women either. He plays a man whose every move is circumscribed by some foolish womanly notion. In Fieldsian myth, marriage, order, codes of behavior, and, above all, temperance are invented by women to fence in the natural man's appetites. It is notable that as Sousé lures his victim, Snoopington, to the Black Pussy Cat Café, he asks the bank examiner whether he has noticed Lompoc's beautiful girls. The examiner harrumphs that he is married and has a grown daughter "eighteen years of age." In other words, marriage has closed his eyes to other women. The man is no man. Sousé, on the other hand, continues muttering under his breath. "That's how I like 'em, seventeen, eighteen . . ." Sousé drugs Snoopington with a Mickey Finn in the Black Pussy Cat Café, half leads, half carries him to a room in the New Old Lompoc House, then either allows him to fall or pushes him out the window of that new old establishment, hauls the bruised and disheveled examiner up the stairs once again, back into the room, and puts him to bed—all because Snoopington's sole desire in the world is to examine the books at the bank where Sousé and his future son-in-law, Og, have made an "unauthorized" loan.

Even this brief summary reveals the Dickensian spirit of Fields, a comedian whose joy in naming things is as great as his joy in the visual joke. Should we be in doubt as to the source of the filmmaker's inspiration, the bank examiner assists us. From his sickbed, the prissy Snoopington worries aloud about his wife. "My poor wife," he moans, "Little Dorrit." But, as it turns out, Sousé has underestimated the bureaucrat's willpower. The examiner somehow manages to crawl from his sickbed and arrive at the bank ready for duty. Although he is obviously woozy and a tad unstable on his feet, Snoopington's pressed suit betrays no sign of his earlier misadventures. The wily Sousé conspires to crush Snoopington's spectacles and render the examiner blind. Sousé succeeds in smashing the glasses under his foot, upon which the examiner opens his briefcase. The camera zooms in on a close shot of its contents. The man has five extra pairs of spectacles neatly lined up within. The eyewear tells all. Driven by duty, this man comes prepared. In the finicky realm of ledgers, numbers, and accounts, he has no rival. We know, however, with absolute certainty, that he will live and die a bank examiner. Sousé, on the other hand, through mad accident and wild connivance, becomes fabulously wealthy. At the end of the movie he is happily ensconced in his mansion, where his formerly abusive family now dotes on him. Fields makes a contented exit. He is off to the Black Pussy Cat Café as of old. His family declares him "a changed man."

Fenced in, stuck on a rung of the social ladder, the Pangbornian man has no appetite for change. Like most children he prefers sameness, routine, consistency. This, too, I understand. Repetition is the essence of meaning. Without it we are lost. But taken to its extreme, a love of system becomes absurd. Franklin Pangborn played a man who worshipped the system in which he found himself, a system ruled by that Manichaean American divinity, its God and its Satan: money. Money haunts Pangborn's character in most of his movies. He does not have much of it himself, but he is victim to its charms, part of its overriding machinery, and overly impressed by its power. The quintessential manager, he's a dupe of the rich. In another Preston Sturges film, *Christmas in July*, Pangborn plays the manager of a department store, eager to please the hero and his girlfriend, who falsely think themselves newly rich and go on a shopping spree. The manager shows them a bed, a piece of furniture outfitted with an elaborate mechanism that will afford them every convenience at the touch of a button. Pangborn unfolds this wonder of American consumerism, and then in a voice at once elevated, proper, and obsequious he says, "And then on the morrow . . ." He presses the proverbial button and the bed collapses back into itself.

I realize that it is not only the character of Pangborn that I am attached to but the fact that he appeared in Hollywood movies during an era when dialogue still played a prominent role in the making of films, when the archaic expression "on the morrow" could be written for a laugh, when W. C. Fields could throw away a line in homage to Little Dorrit, when a Weenie King could soliloquize on his love for dirt, cyclones, and disease. It is rare now that a studio movie gives us much dialogue of any sort, and when it does, it is inevitably a language without much history, a language afraid of reference lest its audience not understand, a language deadened by the politics of the committee and the test screening. And as I bemoan this, I know full well that studios ran then and run now on an idea that is populist at heart: to get the largest number of people into the theater to see a movie that will please all or almost all—eggheads and curmudgeons excluded. But even in bad movies of the Pangborn period, talk played a larger role than it does now. I miss talk in the movies.

And the fact is that when I leave my house in Brooklyn and I listen to people in the streets, to their locutions and their diction, to their phrases and sentences, they bear little resemblance to what I hear on-screen in "big" movies. People in my neighborhood are prey to all kinds of grandiose expressions, to malapropisms, and to flourishes of the tongue. The other day I heard a woman say to another woman, "He's nothing but a little," she paused, "a little blurb." A man sitting outside the Korean grocery in my neighborhood was musing aloud about the word *humanism*. "You call that humanism, humanistic, human beingness," he roared at anyone who would listen. Years ago, an old man sat in the Fifty-ninth Street subway station and sang out a sequence of beautiful words: "Coppelia, Episcopalian, echolalia . . ." He had a resonant, stentorian voice that still rings in my ears. Once in La Bagel Delight, a local deli, I garbled my words and asked the man behind the counter for a cinnamon *Reagan* bagel. He looked at me and said, "We don't have any of those, but I'll give you a pumper-

Nixon." Wit and wonder live on in everyday speech. They merely go untapped in Hollywood.

The truth is that the world and our fantasies often overlap. Franklin Pangborn's character, that meticulous, preening stuffed shirt, is not only a fiction of the screen. Once, with my own eyes, I saw his reincarnation. Several years ago, my husband and I were in Paris. He had some business there, and we were put up in a grand old hotel near the Louvre. It happened that the French actor Gerard Depardieu had taken it into his head to meet my husband, and a rendezvous was arranged in the hotel lobby. Depardieu's name had well before then become synonymous with French movies. It seemed to me that every French film I saw had that man in it. His fame was incontrovertible. The actor entered the hotel. Unlike many movie stars, he did not disappoint off the screen. He is a very large man, a formidable man, and he burns with energy. Clad in a leather jacket, his motorcycle helmet tucked under his arm, he headed toward us, his gait determined but galumphing. Depardieu exuded nothing so much as testosterone, an unvarnished, out-of-the-street maleness that, to be honest, bowled me over. From the corner of my eye, I noticed the manager of the hotel notice who had just entered his establishment. Visible but controlled excitement could be seen on his features. His face made it eminently clear that the closer Depardieu came to us, the higher our status rose in that hotel. His sharp eyes never left the celebrity. The actor arrived at our table in the lobby. He greeted my husband, the two other people with us, and me. I remember that he boomed my name with pleasure, shook my hand with the powerful grip I had expected, and seated himself. The maître d'hôtel rushed over. Posture erect, chin up, scrupulously attired in his expensive dark suit and elegant tie, he tried to maintain his equanimity. He did not succeed. In his joy he began to flap his arms just a little, as if he were trying to propel himself off the ground. Then, with a dignified nod of his head in the direction of the famous one, he asked him for his drink order. Mr. Depardieu casually ordered a glass of red wine. The manager turned abruptly on his heels and speed-walked off to get it. He did not take anybody else's order. He forgot us.

As I watched him leave, I thought of Franklin Pangborn. Franklin Pangborn had been reborn in that hotel lobby, and I was there to witness his inspired silliness. The poor manager behaved in a ridiculous manner, but I felt sorry for him, too. He had breached his own rigorous standards of etiquette and had made a fool of himself. But then we all make fools of our-selves from time to time. And that, I suppose, is at the bottom of this rambling but sincerely felt tribute to the Pangbornian.

1998

Eight Days in a Corset

LAST SUMMER, I WORKED AS AN EXTRA IN THE FILM VERSION of Henry James's novel *Washington Square*. I am not an actress. Agnieszka Holland, the director, is a friend of my husband's and mine, and the person she was really interested in was our daughter, Sophie, who was cast as one of Mrs. Almond's children. Under a blasting June sun, Sophie and I arrived in Baltimore for a fitting. Sophie was dressed first, and she looked as pretty as a young heroine in any book. One of the two wardrobe women handed me a corset, a hoopskirt, and a petticoat, which I put on, and then she tightened my stays. They searched for a dress long enough to fit me, and I climbed into it in front of a long, wide mirror in the changing room.

Within a few minutes, I felt faint. I began to suffer from the feeling I always have when I am faint—acute embarrassment. This time there was the added burden of fear: that I would crash to the floor in front of my eight-year-old daughter. I began to sway, dropped, but did not black out. I wish I could say that they cried, "Loosen her stays!" hurried out for smelling salts, and waved my ashen face with a fan. But they didn't.

They kindly brought me water and grapes as I recovered. I joked about filling the role too well, about becoming in a matter of minutes the classic image of a swooning nineteenth-century lady, and yet I don't believe it was the corset. I had almost fainted in front of a mirror once before—in a yoga class. That time I was wearing dance tights and a sweatshirt. My teacher was correcting my posture, and without warning I collapsed and found myself breathing deeply with my head between my knees.

Mirrors are where I check myself—for parsley stuck in my teeth, for blemishes and dirty hair—where I ponder which shoes go with which dress. But every once in a while, they become something more than that—the site of a body I know will eventually give up the ghost. As in fairy tales and folklore, the mirror displays for an instant my ghost double, and I don't like seeing her. It is a moment when I am a stranger to myself. But a foreign reflection in a mirror is not always a shock. There is something appealing about transformations, and clothes are the fastest route to leaping out of your own life and into someone else's. The whalebone corset I wore for eight days catapulted me into another time and another aesthetic, and I liked it.

The corset is a vilified article of clothing. It was and is blamed for a host of feminine miseries, both physical and spiritual, for ruining women's bodies and for closing their minds. It is interesting to note, however, that while women wore them, it was male doctors who led the campaign against the corset. Most women were for it. In the twentieth century, feminists joined physicians and attacked the garment as crippling. No doubt there were women who, in the heat of summer or in front of a parlor fire in winter, lost consciousness in corsets too tightly laced for their own good. But wearing mine day in and day out, I fell prey to its charms. Wearing a corset is a little like finding oneself in a permanent embrace, a hug around the middle that goes on and on. This is pleasant and vaguely erotic—a squeeze that lasts.

But the feeling of a corset is only part of its effect. Like all clothing, more than anything else, it is an idea. In this case it promotes an idea of a woman's body as radically different from a man's. In the summer of 1986, I traveled in Asia with my three sisters and we visited both a Buddhist monastery and a Buddhist nunnery in the mountains of Taiwan. Those monks and nuns looked *exactly* alike—small, trim, hairless bodies with shaved heads. The monks had orange robes, the nuns white. Had they all stripped naked and stood together, the difference between them would have been ridiculously small, would have been no more nor less than what the difference truly is—genital variation and a few secondary sexual characteristics in the chest and hips. The truth about clothes, hairdos, and makeup had never hit me so hard. The cultural trappings of sex are overwhelming. We make them and live them and are them.

The corset takes the difference between men and women and runs wild with it. The inward slope of a woman's waist becomes extreme, and the tension of lacing the waist pushes the breasts upward. Suddenly, I had new breasts. I did not know how much my body had changed until I saw a photograph of myself in costume and marveled at this addition to my anatomy. The corset leaves most of the breasts free and does not cover the genitals. By lodging itself securely between upper and lower body parts, its effect is to articulate them more sharply and define them as separate erotic zones. The corset helped to create a notion of femininity, and the lines it produced have gone in and out of fashion ever since. If I had never seen a corset before or had never imagined myself in one, it probably wouldn't have had much power, but I grew up on nineteenth-century novels and studied the illustrations in Dickens and Thackeray very closely. Snug in my corset, with a body I had never seen before, I became an illustration to myself of a world I had only read about.

The corset did not live alone, however. In the 1860s, the time during which James set his novel, it was joined by other garments essential to the American bourgeois woman: the hoopskirt and the petticoat padded at the hips. The padding exaggerates the tiny waist created by the corset, and the hoop turns a woman into a kind of walking bell. The hoop's threat is real. You sit, and if you are not careful, it flies up over your head. No one can scrub floors in a hoop. If you're wearing one, it's a sign that during the day you are *never* on your knees. It is possible to arrange flowers in a hoop, lift a teacup, read a book, and point out tasks to your servants. The hoop was a sign of class; its restriction meant luxury. Like the Chinese aristocrat with fingernails a yard long, it tells a story: "I do not work for money." And I did notice among some of the extras a touch of envy among those who were cast as maids in sad, gray dresses for those of us who swished along in our private balloons. Our movements might have been hampered, but we took up a lot of space, and that space, I realized, was a matter of pride.

And then, alas, they did my hair. I liked the corset. I was amused by my petticoats and laughed at the hoop, except when I had to back slowly into a bathroom stall wearing the crazy thing. (Women of the period did not back into stalls. Their underwear was open, and they could pee standing up. Yes, like a man.) The hairdo was another matter. I am six feet tall. I was forty-one years old. When they had finished with me, I looked like a giraffe in ringlets. The only people in the world who come by ringlets naturally are babies. During that period every woman who could afford to be curled was—young, old, and in between. It was baby fashion, and to my mind it made every woman over twenty look ridiculous. Like the hourglass figure, the longing for infancy through garments or hairdos comes and goes. The short shifts of the sixties were a movement back to childhood, as were the big eyes and ringlets of the same period. Only a few years ago I read about the fashion among teenagers and young club-goers to drape pacifiers around their necks after they had squeezed themselves into baby clothes. Female Peter Pans.

In other words, the idea is what matters. Clothes give us insight into culture and its wishes, and into individuals and their desires. More than who you are, clothes articulate what you want to be. Ringlets were hard for me, because I like to think of myself as a grown-up, because I strive for a certain dignity in my apparel, but that dignity is no more than a message I want to communicate, and who knows if it is successful? I love clothes and have often pined for them—the beautiful dress or coat in the window. My desire is for the transformation I imagine will take place, a kind of enchantment of my own body.

Children are closer to fantastic transformations than adults, closer to the spell of costume and the change that comes from illusion, but we all are prone to it, and hiding behind the silk nightgown or the stockings or the pin-striped suit is a story we have heard and repeated to ourselves. These stories are often clichés, worn narratives we hold close to our hearts. I am changing into the silk nightgown, have brushed my hair and pinched my cheeks. I walk into the bedroom and there he is—the hero, Clark Gable or William Powell, depending on my mood. He turns, gasps, "You look . . ." Fill in the blank. Whatever the words are, it is never: "You look like yourself."

Any meaningful piece of clothing is part of a broader cultural story. Years ago I went to a Halloween party as a man. In a borrowed suit, my face wiped clean of all makeup, and my hair hidden under a hat, I looked at myself in a mirror and was unprepared for the change. Women flirt with men's clothing all the time, but when you go all the way, the result is striking. I felt manly. My stride lengthened. My manner changed. It was easy to play at being a man, as easy as playing at being a woman. The suit unleashed a fantasy of maleness I heartily enjoyed. Another time, I was walking down a dark street in New York on my way to a large party. I was in my early twenties then and experimented occasionally with wild attire. In a red jumpsuit and heels, which added several inches to my already towering frame, I passed a man who began spewing insults at me. I kept walking. It took several seconds for me to digest what was happening. The man had mistaken me for a transvestite. The experience, both comic and sad, gave me sudden insight into the venom that appearances can produce, not to speak of the often hazy line between femininity and its parodic double.

Every once in a while, a piece of clothing jumps out of one culture and into another. I spent three months in Thailand in 1975 as a student, and I vividly remember seeing a gang of motorcycle toughs roaring through the streets of Chiang Mai in the rain, wearing shower caps. Several of those caps were decorated with flowers and other beacons of feminine adornment. I was amazed, but nobody else was. My cultural associations didn't apply. The shower cap had been born again somewhere else with a totally different signification.

While it is true that certain individuals are fixed on an idea that rigidly determines them—whether it be "I do not care about clothes at all" or "I am a sex goddess"—most of us have or have had over time many different dreams. I own a black dress that reminds me of Audrey Hepburn. I do not suffer from the delusion that I look like Audrey Hepburn in that dress, but her exquisite form wrapped in Givenchy has bewitched it nevertheless, and her magic is part of my pleasure in wearing it. Movies and books are strong drugs to clothes lovers. Katharine Hepburn striding along in trousers, Lana Turner in a towel, Claudette Colbert in a man's pajama top, Marilyn Monroe in anything. Tolstoy lavished his attention on the details of women's clothes and bodies, on Natasha at her first ball and Ellen's white shoulders above her low-cut gown. Jane Eyre's plain dress is a tonic against the frippery of the silly females who visit Rochester. And all these images are taken from moments in larger stories that captivate us, stories about people who are living out their lives and their romantic entanglements, both comic and tragic.

My daughter dresses up. She is a rich woman, then a poor one, starving in the streets. She is an old peasant woman selling apples. She is on the phone saying, "Let's have lunch," in an English accent. She sashays down the stairs snapping her gum and practicing her Brooklyn voice. She is wearing my shoes and singing "Adelaide's Lament." She is always somebody else. My husband says I have two personas at least, the stooped four-eyed scholar and the elegant lady. One lives more at home. The other goes out. Thinking collapses my body, and I forget what I look like anyway. In a good dress, I stand up straight and never slump. I live up to the dress I know I am wearing even though I do not see myself wearing it. Others see me more often than I see myself. My family knows what I look like better than I do. I offer the mirror a placid face like an inanimate statue, and from time to time that frozen image may frighten me. But I also laugh a lot and smile. I wrinkle my face in concern, and I wave my hands when I talk, and this I never see.

In the end, wearing clothes is an act of the imagination, an invention of self, a fiction. Several years ago, I was sitting in the Carlyle Hotel with my husband having a drink. I was wearing a beautiful dress. I remember that he looked across the table at me with pleasure and said, "When you were a little girl growing up in the sticks of Minnesota, did you ever imagine you would be sitting in this elegant hotel wearing that extraordinary dress?"

And I said, "Yes." Because of course, I did.

1996

Being a Man

IN MY WAKING LIFE I'M A WOMAN, BUT SOMETIMES IN MY dreams I'm a man. My masculinity is rarely a question of simple anatomy. I don't discover that I've sprouted a penis and am growing a beard, but rather I realize that I'm a man in the same moment I am troubled by the vague memory that I was once a woman. My sex becomes important in the dream only when it's called into doubt. It is doubt, not certainty, that produces first the question of my sexual identity and second the need to be one thing or the other, man or woman. Although it is now fashionable to dismiss dreams as meaningless neurological chatter, I've discovered too much in my own sleep to believe that. It is obvious that my dreams of manliness, which turn on a moment of confusion, illuminate recesses of my own muddled psyche, but I also think they can be used as a key to understanding the larger cultural terrain where the boundary between femininity and masculinity is articulated.

Most of us accept the biological realities of our sex and live with them more or less comfortably, but there are times when the body feels like a limitation. For a woman it may come when she hears a note of condescension in a man's voice and she must confront the fact that it isn't what she has said that has produced this tone; it's her sex. Of course, such a moment isn't easy to analyze because every social encounter is laden with the unsaid and the unseen. Two people inevitably create a third realm between them in which sex is only one of the myriad forces at work, and yet, like envy, resentment, class snobbery, or racism, sexual prejudice can be detected like an odor in the room, and if the smell gets too strong, it prompts a fantasy of escape: What would he have said if he had seen me as a man? I'm sure that my dreams of maleness are at least partly about escaping the cultural expectations that burden femininity, but I also think they are something more complex, that the dreams recognize a truth that there is a man in me as well as a woman and that this duality is in fact part of being human, but not one that is always easy to reconcile.

In my dreams, my real body doesn't restrain me. I fly and have powers of telekinesis. I've grown fur, suffered gaping wounds, lost my teeth, and shed enough blood to drown in. When I write fiction, I also leave my real body behind and become someone else, another woman or a man if I wish. For me, making art has always been a kind of conscious dreaming. The material for a story comes not from what I know but from what I don't know, from impulses and images that often seem to happen without my directives, a strange process altogether and one that is put in play when I become another person in my work. And yet the act of writing consists of one thing only—putting words on a page to be read by someone else. In the end, the words are everything and, strictly speaking, they are sexless. In English, unlike many other languages, our nouns don't even have gender, but it's interesting to ask whether a text can be male or female and what would make it one or the other.

Every parent and anyone who's spent time with young children knows that sexual identity takes a while to fix itself and that toddlers rarely know if they are boys or girls. When my daughter was three, she asked my husband whether she would get a penis when she grew up. She posed this question during a period in her life I call the tutu-party-shoe phase, an era of glitter and gold, rhinestone tiaras and plastic high heels. While the little boys were puffing out their chests and playing superheroes, my daughter was tripping around the house like a mad, rather smudged version of Titania. At the same age, the daughter of a friend of mine donned a platinum Marilyn Monroe wig and refused to take it off. She ate, played, went to the park, the toilet, and bed under the increasingly ratty white peruke, which, according to her mother, made her look more like Rumplestiltskin than a blond bombshell. However comic they may look to adults, children play hard at finding out what they are—boys or girls—and they live the difference through an often furious imaginary drama of sex roles. Despite the optimism of some researchers, where biology ends and culture begins is probably a question beyond science. Even infants, whose borderless existence makes the question of sexual identity seem absurd from the inside, have been born into a world in which the boy/girl question is crucial from the outside, is the first question asked after birth: "Is it a boy or a girl?" In other words, before they know, we know. And what we know is part of a vast symbolic landscape in which the lines are drawn between one thing and another in the linguistic act of naming. Once children feel sure of themselves as either boys or girls, the Zorro capes, Superman outfits, crowns, and princess costumes are replaced by more androgynous clothing. The external trappings of femininity and masculinity can be discarded at the moment the knowledge of sexual identity becomes internal, and part of that inner certainty happens in language. A six-year-old can usually state with confidence that he or she is a boy or girl, will grow up to be a man or a woman, and, barring an operation, will not change sex along the way. At the same time, the wider meanings of femininity and masculinity are far more ambiguous. *Male* and *female* are words that carry associations so dense, so old, so public, but also so private, that drawing a clear line between the two is riddled with difficulty. It must be said, however, that the categories male and female are very much alive in the language and are laden with our own deep cultural and personal histories that continue to evolve and change and that it is wildly naïve to suppose that dropping *chairman* for *chairperson*, for example, will purge language of its sexual connotations.

We were four daughters in my family. My parents had the name Lars ready before each birth, but it turned out that they had to wait a generation for him. My sister's first son was named Lars in honor of our grandfather and the phantom Hustvedt boy who was never born. I have often thought it was easier that we were all girls. Had there been a boy, we might have been compared and opposed to him, and the differences might have confined all of us. We were born in pairs. I was first. Then, nineteen months later, my sister Liv was born. A gap of five years followed before Asti appeared, and only fifteen months later Ingrid arrived. The four of us were very close and loyal to one another as children and remain devoted friends as adults, something we have more or less taken for granted. My husband, on the other hand, has always regarded our harmony as both remarkable and somewhat puzzling.

Why are there so few conflicts among us? When Liv and I were very young, we liked disaster games—shipwreck, tornado, flood, and war. Liv was always John, and I was always Mary, which usually meant that John got to save Mary. I liked being rescued, and in life as well as in play, my sister was the brave one, not I, and on several occasions she defended me from the assaults of other children, even though I was her older sister. The two youngest girls were similarly cast. Asti generally preferred the role of girl when playing, and Ingrid liked to be the boy. Liv and Ingrid took up horsemanship and both became amateur rodeo champions. Later, Liv went into business. Ingrid became an architect. Asti and I both ended up in graduate school, she in French, I in English.

Although not nearly full enough, this brief sketch helps to explain why ten years into our marriage, my husband sat up in bed one morning and said to me, "I've understood everything. You're the woman. Liv's the man. Asti's the girl, and Ingrid is the boy." We are all grown up now, are all married and all have children, but my sisters and I recognized in that statement a truth about our family that had never been articulated by anyone before. Despite the fact that we were all girls, we established a pattern of alternating feminine and masculine qualities among the sisters. It's notable that it was the younger girl in each pair who adopted the more masculine role, which helped compensate for the deficit in age. The effect was simple. Within each pair, the rivalry typical between siblings of the same sex who are nearly the same age was greatly diminished. It's impossible to compete if you're not playing the same game.

A number of years after that succinct assessment of me and my sisters, I was reading a book of collected papers by D. W. Winnicott, the English pediatrician and psychoanalyst, and came across a lecture called "On the Split-off Male and Female Elements," which he delivered to the British Psycho-Analytical Society in 1966. He introduces the subject by saying, "As a basis for the idea that I wish to give here I suggest that creativity is one of the common denominators of men and women. In another language, however, creativity is the prerogative of women, and in yet another language, it is a masculine feature. It is the last of the three that concerns me here." Winnicott goes on to explain that one day during a conversation with a male patient, he felt that he was hearing a girl and said: "I am listening to a girl. I know perfectly well that you are a man but I am listening to a girl. . . ." The patient replied, "If I were to tell someone about this girl, I would be called mad." Winnicott took the next step: "It was not that *you* told this to anyone; it is *I* who see the girl and hear the girl talking, when actually there is a man on my couch. The mad person is *myself*." The patient answered, "I myself could never say (knowing myself to be a man) 'I am a girl.' I am not mad in that way. But you said it, and you have spoken to both parts of me."

Winnicott's interpretation of this extraordinary dialogue (which he emphasizes has nothing to do with homosexuality) hinges on the understanding that the man's late mother, who already had an older son when she gave birth to her second child, had wanted a girl and had insisted on seeing the second baby as the wrong sex. The reversal was caused by the mother's "madness," not the son's. The mother's wish was a lie, which in turn created a painful ghost in the son—the desired daughter. My sisters and I didn't suffer from the roles we played in our family the way Winnicott's patient did, and it's probably because my mother wasn't deluded. She loved her babies as girls. I am inclined to think that what happened with us came later and is connected to my father. We four still laugh about the fact that when my father wanted help in the garage he usually asked for Liv or Ingrid.

I spent six years writing a book in which the narrator is a seventy-year-old man named Leo Hertzberg. When I began the novel, I felt some anxiety about embodying a man and speaking in a male voice. After a short time, that nervousness fell away, but it became clear to me that I was doing something different, that this speaker lived inside himself in a different way from me, and yet to *be* him, I was drawing on a masculine part of myself. I've played with sexual ambiguity in my work before. The heroine of my first novel, *The Blindfold*— a book also written in the first person—cuts her hair, takes on the name of a boy in a story she has translated, and wanders the streets of New York dressed in a man's suit. While I was writing that book, I knew Iris had to put on the suit, but I never knew why except that her cross-dressing was connected to her translation of the German novella *The Brutal Boy*, a movement from one language into another, and that by pretending to be a man she loses some vulnerability and gains some power, which she desperately needs. It has never occurred to me until now that taking on a masculine position as a survival technique has roots in my own family, that in the suit Iris lives out the duality and uncertainty of my dreams, and that when she reinvents herself as a male character she is finally able to imagine her own rescue. As "Klaus" she also speaks differently, uses profanity, and adopts a confident swagger she associates with men. Not long ago, I met a psychiatrist who told me that she gives *The Blindfold* to a number of her female patients. "It doesn't make them worse?" I asked her, only half-joking. "No," she said. "It helps for them to see that the boundaries are important." Iris's cross-dressing is defensive, an escape from the openness, fragility, and boundlessness she connects to her femininity.

Being Leo was not an act of translation. After a while, I began to hear him. I heard a man. It's probably impossible to explain where he came from, but I'm convinced that I drew from the experience of listening to the men I have loved, my father and my husband, in particular, but also from others who have been crucial to my intellectual life—those disembodied male voices inside the innumerable books I have read over the years. Their words are in me, but then so are the words of women writers. Jane Austen, Emily and Charlotte Brontë, George Eliot, Emily Dickinson, Gertrude Stein, Djuna Barnes have also altered my imagination, and yet I'm not talking about sexual difference in terms of real bodies but am reiterating Winnicott, ". . . I was now no longer thinking of boys and girls or men and women," he writes, "but I was thinking in terms of the male and female elements that belong to each." After years of experience, Winnicott learned to listen to his patients in a way that transcended anatomy. Reading means not seeing the writer. Marian Evans became George Eliot to hide her sex, and it worked for a while. Flaubert's declaration *"Madame Bovary, c'est moi"* is as earnest as anything he ever said.

As a reader of books, I'm convinced that words have an almost magical power to generate, not only more words but fleeting images, emotions, and memories. Certain novels and poems have had a power to unearth raw and unknown parts of myself, have been like mirrors I never knew existed. In every book, the writer's body is missing, and this absence turns the page into a place where we are truly free to listen to the man or woman who is speaking. When I write a book, I am also listening. I hear the characters talk as if they were outside me rather than inside me. In one book, I heard a young woman who played at being a man; in another, I heard a man. In my dreams, I find myself pulled between the two sexes, wondering which one I am. Not knowing bothers me, but when I write, that same ambivalence becomes my liberation, and I am free to inhabit both men and women and to tell their stories.

2003

Leaving Your Mother

IT WAS VISITOR'S WEEKEND AT CAMP, AND I HAD MY TWELVE-year-old daughter, Sophie, in my arms as we sat on her bunk talking. From across the cabin I heard a girl moan, "I wish my mom would come. Where is she?" Another girl lying flat on her back in bed complained to the ceiling, "Yeah, I want to sit on *my* mom's lap." They were still waiting for their mothers to arrive. When the parents left that day, some children cried; some didn't. Some clung desperately to their mothers and fathers. Others offered them only a quick, perfunctory hug. A veteran spectator of visiting weekend told me he could always spot the divorced parents, because when the mother or father said good-bye to the child, the boyfriend, girlfriend, or stepparent would stand apart—at a respectful distance of at least ten paces. Good-byes initiate separations, and it isn't easy to part with one's mother and father, even though we all do in the end. My husband likes to say that our job as parents is to raise children who are strong enough to go off and do well without us.

When I was seven and my sister Liv was five, we bid good-bye to our mother and father and took the train to Chicago with my great uncle David. He wasn't our real uncle but my grandfather's cousin, and in 1962 he was already an old man, probably in his early eighties. Uncle David had always been a part of our lives, and Liv and I were very fond of him. He had left Norway when he was twenty-two to make his fortune in America and ended up outside Chicago, where he had worked as a carpenter. Uncle David was fun. He walked for miles every day, played strenuous games with us, and showed his affection by giving us sudden, fierce hugs, which despite the fact that they were enthusiastic were also decidedly uncomfortable.

I don't remember feeling anything but excitement as my sister and I and Uncle David stepped onto the train, and I have no conscious memory of saying good-bye to my parents. Liv and I felt that the trip was to be the adventure of our lives, and we embraced it wholeheartedly. It began well. We were sitting in our big train seats across from Uncle David when suddenly two men, with red bandanas tied over their noses, came running through the car. In hot pursuit behind them came two policemen with guns. Amazed, Liv and I asked Uncle David who those men were. Unruffled, he said, "Probably baggage robbers." My sister and I were delighted: real robbers.

Uncle David lived with his unmarried daughter, a schoolteacher, whom we called Aunt Harriet. Their house was dark as I remember it. Maybe the curtains were often pulled or maybe the windows didn't get much light—I don't know—but it was an umbral place and it smelled old. The first night of our visit, Aunt Harriet told us to "go upstairs and take your bath now." Liv and I looked at each other, walked up the stairs, opened the bathroom door, entered the room, and stood staring at the bathtub. We had never taken a bath alone. We had never turned on the water in a bathtub. Our mother filled the bath. She washed our hair, and she warmed towels in the dryer to prevent us from catching a chill. In the winter, my father would often wrap us in those warm towels, lift us up into his arms, and place us in front of a fire. I remember clearly that Liv and I conferred about what we should do. We had been given an order. It never occurred to us to disobey it, nor did it occur to us to ask for help. We did take a bath—in cold, shallow water. It lasted about two minutes.

During the days that followed, we never left Highwood. When Aunt Harriet went off to work, Uncle David entertained us. A high point of the visit, which I remember with burning clarity, was the afternoon Uncle David beckoned us into his room. As my sister and I watched, he reclined on his bed in a luxurious manner, shoes on the bedspread, and with great ceremony extracted a bank note from his wallet. We leaned forward to look at it. It was a hundred-dollar bill. We had never seen so much money in one place before. "Whenever you need one of these," he said, "you can come to me." Liv and I were deeply impressed.

I'm not sure when I started missing home and longing for my parents, but I suspect it was after only a couple of days. The entire visit couldn't have lasted more than two weeks. What is interesting to me now is that I didn't articulate the feeling to myself. I didn't say, "I want to go home," or, "I'm homesick." At the same time, I had a strong sense that Liv and I shared our feelings, whether we spoke of them or not. We stuck together, discussed how different Uncle David's was from what we were used to, but we didn't cry or ask that anything be changed. Then I wrote a letter home. I believe that it was a cheerful letter, that I gave a report to my mother and father about our doings in Highwood, but with the letter I sent a drawing of Jesus. The Bible stories I had learned in Sunday school had had a great effect on me, and at seven I was a pious child. God and angels and miracles and the terrible story of the crucifixion inhabited my inner world, and it came into my head to draw a picture of Jesus praying to God, his father, in the garden at Gethsemane before he is taken away and crucified. I worked on it very hard. I thought it was the best, most beautiful drawing I had ever made. Christ was kneeling in prayer, and I think he was wearing a blue robe. I folded it up and sent it off with my news.

My mother took one look at the drawing and decided to take a train to Chicago. For me, the message of the drawing was entirely unconscious, but my mother read it correctly. It said: "Take this cup from me." I still remember the sight of my mother at the train station, the sound of her voice, the feeling of her body, and the smell of her perfume when Liv and I threw ourselves into her open arms.

That trip and my mother's arrival have remained as vivid for me as any event in my childhood. Uncle David and Aunt Harriet didn't tell us that my mother was coming. She later told me that she had been against this plan, but there was little she could do to dissuade them from the idea of a surprise. Because we were in the dark, her appearance struck us both as a magical event, like a wish granted in a fairy tale. This enchanted quality was furthered by the fact that I had called out to my mother, without knowing I had done it, and she, endowed with what I regarded as supernatural penetration into the recesses of my soul, answered the call and appeared.

Because our mothers are our first loves, because it is through them that we begin to find ourselves as separate beings in a new world, they have, for better or for worse, immense power. Liv and I were kindly treated by our relatives, and yet the visit remains in both of our minds as our first venture into a strange environment. I remember the alien bedcovers and the odd cereal bowls. I even remember the yellow-ing grass in the yard, as though it, too, had been touched by another reality. Through experience most adults lose that in-tense feeling of the unfamiliar—of being *not home*. Of course, had our mother been with us, Liv and I would not have felt the change so strongly. The truth is that the idea of home and the idea of our mother and father were inseparable.

At seven I was more than old enough to have a grip on the real, to feel certain that I would see my parents again, and yet I longed for them. My parents were like the ground under my feet. Without them, I felt suspended and unsure of my steps. Anyone who has ever had a baby knows that an eight-month-old, for example, is *not* sure you will return, that leaving the room is enough to set off a wild protest. I remember that when my daughter had just learned to walk and I talked on the phone, she would suddenly become demanding. You don't have to leave the room to leave a child. My desire to talk to somebody else was enough to create anxiety and irritation in her. When I was off the phone and completely available to her, she would often wander off, suddenly very busy and seem-ingly unaware of my presence. There's the rub. A child's true independence is the product of a strong, reassuring parental presence, and it is that presence that we take with us when we walk out the door for good.

Although I work at home, I have left my daughter more of-ten over the years than my mother left me. When Sophie was four, I went on a book tour in Germany for two and a half weeks. She stayed at home with her father and my mother, both of whom adore her, and they took very good care of her. When I returned, she clung to me but was decidedly cool to my mother. It doesn't take a brilliant psychologist to know that it wasn't my mother she was angry at but me for leaving

her, and yet the replacement mother took the rap. Many step-
parents have found themselves in the same position—as the
targets of displaced anger. For two years after that, whenever
I traveled, my daughter would look up at me and say, "You're
not going to Germany, are you, Mommy?" *Germany*, a country
she would never have been able to find on a map, became the
sign for her of missing me, and while I am glad I went away
for my work, the unhappiness of my own child who was left in
the care of people she loved and who loved her suggests that
even what might be regarded as an ideal separation leaves a
trace. When Sophie was nine, I traveled to Germany again for
my second novel. By then the name of the country had lost its
mournful connotations and she was only delighted to be with
her grandmother during my absence and afterward. The nine-
year-old was far better equipped emotionally to understand
my departure than the four-year-old had been.

It is well known that small children often take a parental
absence personally, that they feel somehow responsible for a
beloved parent being gone. All little children love their parents and at the same time resent their omnipotence, and if the
parent disappears, they can't help assuming that their aggressive feelings might have had something to do with it. And if
they are feeling vulnerable about their greatest love, they may
take out their anger elsewhere—on a safer object. I knew a little boy who, while his father was away, repeatedly called his
beloved uncle "Stupid." All dads were suspect. When his father returned, the boy beat the parent he had missed with his
small fists, before giving way to a passionate embrace and
tears.

The normal pains of love and anger most children suffer
when separated from a parent are usually repaired when the
parent returns. Some separations can't be helped. A child or

parent has to be hospitalized for sickness or an injury, for example. In his book *Thinking About Children*, D. W. Winnicott, the English pediatrician and psychoanalyst, tells the story of a four-year-old girl whom he treated in the hospital for possible tuberculosis. "She is a solemn little girl," he writes, "and the joy of life is not in her." Winnicott then discovered that when she was two years old the child had been hospitalized for diphtheria. She had been taken to the hospital while she was *asleep* and woke up in strange surroundings with strange people in the room, and then her mother was forbidden to visit her for three months! One can only imagine that child's despair at finding herself once again in a hospital bed. Winnicott adds, "Possibly her removal from home will be found to have been a great trauma to emotional development. I cannot say."

Winnicott is typically honest. We can only tell a story backward, not forward, but at the very least we must understand that as parents our comings and goings, our presences and absences, are a fragile business. It is well known that children who are repeatedly abandoned or lobbed from one caretaker to another often suffer developmental problems, both cognitive and behavioral, and sometimes what might have been love becomes rage. In the second volume of his classic work, *Attachment and Loss*, John Bowlby quotes from two case studies of teenage boys who killed their mothers. One boy said, "I couldn't stand to have her leave me." Another, who put a bomb in his mother's suitcase as she boarded a plane, said simply, "I decided that she would never leave me again."

The four-year-old who punches his dad for leaving him and the teenagers who commit matricide may appear to be creatures from different planets, but the difference may well be one of degree, not quality. Traumatic separations from parents have long been connected to delinquency, and if physical separation is reinforced by a parent's emotional distance or rejection, the damage to a child may be irreversible.

As I sat and listened to those girls at my daughter's camp bemoan the belated appearance of their mothers, I remembered how long childhood is, how a summer can feel like a year, and a year like a decade. I remembered the trip to Chicago, the hundred-dollar bill, the magical arrival of my mother, and the fact that on the train to Chicago, Liv and I didn't feel the slightest twinge of fear when we saw those baggage robbers rush past us, but the sight of that empty bathtub, without a mother to fill it, caused us considerable alarm. In short, I remembered myself as a child. Looking at my daughter, who is now on the brink of adolescence, I couldn't help feeling that I should keep my memories alive, that if I remember the sometimes bitter trials of being a teenager, both she and I will better negotiate our inevitable separation, the one that will initiate the adventure of her own life, a life she will make alone.

1999

Living with Strangers

IN RURAL MINNESOTA WHERE I GREW UP, IT WAS THE CUSTOM to greet everyone you met on the road, whether you knew the person or not, with a "hi." A dull, muttered, uninflected "hi" was entirely acceptable, but the word had to be spoken. Passing someone in silence wasn't only rude; it could lead to accusations of snobbery—the worst possible sin in my small corner of the egalitarian state.

When I moved to New York City in 1978, I quickly discovered what it meant to live among hordes of strangers and how impractical and unsound it would be to greet all of them. In my two-room apartment on West 109th Street, I heard the ceiling creak as my upstairs neighbor paced his floor. I listened to the howling battles of the couple that lived below me, their raging voices punctuated by thuds, bangs, and the sound of breaking glass. My single view took in the back wall of a building that stood perhaps ten yards away. Lying in my bed at night, I sometimes watched the two young men who lived across the air shaft as they lounged in the light of their window dressed only in their underwear. On the sidewalk, I was jostled, bumped, and elbowed as I negotiated the crowds.

On the subway, I found myself in intimate contact with people I didn't know, my body pressed so tightly against them, I could smell their hair oils, perfumes, and sweat. In my former life, such closeness belonged exclusively to boyfriends and family. It didn't take long for me to absorb the unwritten code of survival in this town—a convention communicated silently but forcefully. This simple law, one nearly every New Yorker subscribes to whenever possible, is: PRETEND IT ISN'T HAPPENING.

This widely applied coping technique is what separates New Yorkers from tourists and seasoned citizens from those who have just come here. An Iranian friend told me that about a week after he had arrived in the city he was traveling uptown on the Second Avenue bus. At Twenty-fourth Street, the door opened for a woman who was wearing nothing but a flimsy bathrobe over her naked body. When she reached the top step, she started feeling her pockets for something and then, with a shocked look on her face, exclaimed, "My token! My token! Oh my God, I must have left it in the other bathrobe!" The driver sighed and waved her onto the bus. My friend had been staring at the woman throughout the scene but was a little ashamed when he understood that he was alone. Nobody else had given the woman a first glance, much less a second.

Last October, I was on the F Train when I noticed a wild-eyed man entering the car. He boomed out a few verses from Revelation and then, in an equally loud voice, began his sermon, informing us that September 11 had been God's just punishment for our sins. I could feel the cold, stiff resistance to his words among the passengers, but not a single one of us turned to look at him.

A couple of weeks ago, after seeing a play at the Brooklyn

Academy of Music, my husband and I walked down the stairs at the Atlantic Avenue station in Brooklyn to wait for the 2 train. I was tired and wanted to sit and noticed a single bench with several empty seats. At the end of that bench sat a man with five or six plastic bags, and although he was perhaps twenty yards away, I did sense that he might be someone to avoid because even at that distance he gave off an aura of silent hostility. Nevertheless, fortified by the presence of my husband, I led the way to the bench. We seated ourselves at its far end, leaving four empty seats between the man and us. After about a minute, he gathered up his bags, shuffled past us, and spat in our direction. His aim wasn't terribly good, but when I looked down I saw a tiny gleaming micro-dot of saliva on my pants knee. We let it go.

These three stories—the bathrobe lady, the fanatical preacher, and the spitter—demonstrate a range of increasingly outrageous behavior that may be dealt with through the *pretend-it-isn't-happening* law. And yet, as my husband pointed out, in the case of the spitter, had there been more saliva on me, he would have felt forced to act. And acting, as everyone in the city knows, can be dangerous. It is usually better to treat the unpredictable among us as ghosts, wandering phantoms who play out their lonely narratives for an audience that appears to be deaf, dumb, and blind.

Taking action may be viewed as courageous or merely stupid, depending on the circumstances and your point of view. A number of years ago, my husband witnessed a memorable exchange on a subway car he was riding to Penn Station. A very tall black man entered the car with a woman dressed in short shorts and high vinyl boots. Both appeared to be under the influence of some powerful pharmaceutical substance. The woman found a place to sit and immediately nodded off.

The man, who was weaving on his feet, took out a cigarette and lit up. Within seconds of that infraction, a little white guy with blond hair, a person probably in his late twenties, wearing a beige trench coat buttoned all the way to his neck, politely demurred. "Excuse me, sir," he said, in a voice that was obviously formed somewhere in the Midwest, "for bothering you, but I want to point out that it's against the law to smoke on the subway." The tall man looked down at his interlocutor, sized him up, paused, and then in deep mellifluous tones, uttered the sentence: "Do you wanna die?"

Most New York stories would have ended there, but not this one. No, the short fellow admitted, he did not want to die, but neither had he finished what he had to say. He persisted, calmly defending the law and its demonstrable rightness. The big man continued puffing on his cigarette as he eyed his opponent with growing amusement. The train stopped. It was time for the smoker to leave, but before he made his exit, he turned to the indefatigable little midwesterner, nodded, and said, "Have a good Dale Carnegie."

That story ended well and with wit, but it carries no moral insight into when to act and when not to act. It is simply one of many ongoing dramas among strangers in the city, who often have little in common except that they all belong to this place. There are moments, however, when a smile or a well-timed comment may change the course of what might otherwise have been a sorry event. For the last year and a half, my fifteen-year-old daughter has been refining the frozen, blank expression that accompanies the Pretend Law, because she spends a couple of hours every day on the subway as she travels from Brooklyn to her school on the Upper West Side in Manhattan and back again. With her Walkman securely over her ears, she feigns deafness when the inevitable stray character comes along and tries a pickup.

One day, she found herself sitting across from "a white guy in his thirties" who stared at her so shamelessly that she felt uncomfortable. She kept her eyes off him and was relieved when the man finally left the car. But, before the train pulled out of the station, the ogler threw himself against the window in front of her and began to pound on the glass. "I love you!" he yelled. "I love you! You're the most beautiful girl I've ever seen in my life!" Deeply embarrassed, Sophie didn't move. Her fellow passengers treated the man as if he were an invisible mute, but as the train began to rumble forward, leaving the histrionic troubadour and his declaration behind, the man sitting next to her looked up from his newspaper and said in a deadpan voice, "It looks like you have an admirer."

Sophie felt better. By breaking the code, the man acknowledged himself as a witness to what, despite the pretense, had been a very public outburst. His understatement not only defined the comedy inherent in the scene; it lifted my daughter out of the solitary misery that comes from being the object of unwanted attention among strangers who collectively participate in a game of erasure. With those few words, and at no cost to himself, he gave her what she needed—a feeling of ordinary human solidarity.

Whatever we might *pretend* not to see or hear or sometimes smell on our sojourns through New York City, most of us actually see, hear, and smell a lot. Behind the mask of oblivion lies alertness (or exhaustion from having to be so alert). Daydreaming on a country road is one thing. Daydreaming on Fifth Avenue with hundreds of other people striding down the same sidewalk is quite another. But because we are so crowded here, active recognition of other people has become mostly a matter of choice. Nevertheless, compliments, insults, banter, smiles, and genuine conversations among strangers are part of the city's noise, its stimulus, its charm. To live in strict accordance to the Pretend Law all the time would be unbearably dull. For us urbanites, both for the born and bred and for converts like me, there is a delight that comes from thinking on our feet, from sizing up situations and making the decision to act or not to act. Most of the time, we insulate ourselves out of necessity, but every once in a while we break through to one another and discover unexpected depths of intelligence or heart or just plain sweetness. And whenever that happens, I am reminded of a truth: Everyone has an inner life that is as large and complex and rich as my own.

Sometimes a brief exchange with an unknown person marks you forever, not because it is profound but because it is uncommonly vivid. Over twenty years ago, I saw a man lying on the sidewalk at Broadway and 105th Street. I guessed that he was in his early sixties, but he may have been younger. Unshaven, filthy, and ragged, he lay on his side in an apparent stupor, clutching a bottle in a torn and wrinkled paper bag. As I walked past him, he suddenly propped himself up on his elbow and called out to me, "Hey, beautiful! Want to have dinner with me?" His question was so loud, so direct, I stopped. Looking down at the man at my feet, I said, "Thank you so much for the invitation, but I'm busy tonight." Without a moment's hesitation, he grinned up at me, lifted the bottle in a mock toast, and said, "Lunch?"

2003

9/11, or One Year Later

1

9/11 HAS BECOME INTERNATIONAL SHORTHAND FOR A CATA-
strophic morning in the United States and the three thousand
dead it left behind. The two numbers have entered the vocabulary of horror: the place names and ideological terms that
are used to designate dozens, hundreds, thousands, sometimes millions of victims—words like My Lai, Oklahoma City,
the Disappeared in Argentina, Sarajevo, Cambodia, Collec-
tivization, the Cultural Revolution, Auschwitz. 9/11 has also
become a threshold and a way of telling time—before and after, pre and post. It has been used to signify the dawn of a new
era, an economic fault line, the onset of war, the presence of
evil in the world, and a loss of American innocence. But for us
New Yorkers, whether we were far from the attacks or close to
them, September 11 remains a more intimate memory. For
weeks afterward, the first question we asked friends and
neighbors whom we hadn't seen since the attacks was: "Is
your family all right? Did you lose anybody?"

The media question "How has life changed in the city since
September 11?" is one that has been reiterated over and over
in the press here and abroad, but it can't be answered by pass-

ing over the day itself. There can be no before and no after, no talk of change, without our stories from that morning and the many mornings that followed, because even for those of us who were lucky and didn't lose someone we loved, September 11 is finally a story of collective trauma and ongoing grief.

Twelve of the thirty firefighters from our local station house in Brooklyn died when the World Trade Center collapsed. Charlie, the owner of the liquor store only a few blocks from our house, a man who has helped me and my husband buy wine for years, lost his sister-in-law. She was a stewardess on the plane that crashed in Pennsylvania. The terrorists slit her throat. Friends of ours who live on John Street were trapped inside their building as the towers fell, their windows shattering from the impact. With help from the police, they finally managed to get out, but as they left, they found themselves stepping over human body parts lying on the ground.

My sister Asti, who lives with her husband and daughter, Juliette, on White Street in Tribeca, was walking south toward P.S. 234, an elementary school only two blocks north of the World Trade Center. She had dropped Juliette off not long before but decided to go and get her after the first plane hit. Asti remembers wondering if she was overreacting. Then she heard the blast of the second plane as it crashed above her. She looked up, saw the gaping hole in the building looming above her, and started to run. By then people were streaming north. She heard someone say, "Oh my God, they're jumping." A woman near her vomited in the street.

My friend Larry, who works at *The Wall Street Journal*, the offices of which were directly across from the towers, escaped from the building and ran until he couldn't run anymore. He stopped to catch his breath, turned, and saw people on fire, jumping from the windows. Hours later, he managed to make his way home across the Brooklyn Bridge. When his panicked wife, Mary, opened the door, she saw a ghost man, covered from head to foot with a fine white powder. After he withdrew from the hug she gave him, Mary noticed that her arms were bleeding from the tiny pieces of pulverized glass that were part of that milky dust.

2

Seeing isn't always believing. Traumatic events are often accompanied by a form of disassociation. What is unfolding before your eyes seems unreal. Although I saw the damage done by the first plane from the window of our house in Brooklyn, I saw the second plane go into the second tower on television. The two pictures I hold in my mind are strangely mismatched. The first has a power that the second doesn't. It has something to do with scale and something to do with unmediated vision. The smoke rising from the familiar skyscraper through my window shocked me. The image on a twenty-one-inch television screen had an alien, almost hallucinatory quality that forced me to say as I watched, "This is true; this is real." Asti, on the other hand, who witnessed the second crash, who heard and saw the horrific destruction only blocks from where she was standing, remained calm. It was only when she had put Juliette to bed that night and saw the plane cut into the building on television that she began to cry.

The problem of direct and mediated images is important to September 11 and its aftermath, not only because most of the world witnessed what happened on television but because the terrorists knew that they were staging a spectacular media event. They knew that in the time that elapsed between the first plane crash and the second television crews would have descended on the scene to record the horrifying image of an airliner entering the second tower and that the tape would be played and replayed for all the world to see, and they knew, too, that it would resemble nothing so much as a big-budget Hollywood disaster movie. A hackneyed fiction remade ad nauseam by the studios was manipulated by the terrorists into grotesque reality. At the same time, it must be said that it took very little imagination on the part of screenwriters to take actual events of terror and enlarge on them to fit the writers' own notions of a thrilling spectacle. September 11 was not unimaginable. We could all imagine it. It's the fact of it that annihilated the fantasy.

On September 12, I was traveling in a subway car during what is normally rush hour on my way to collect my fourteen-year-old daughter, Sophie, who had been stranded overnight on the Upper West Side near her school. There were only a few of us in that car—myself and five or six other silent, stunned passengers who had decided that a trip was necessary. Because the regular line had been damaged by the attacks, I left one train to find another and noticed a large poster for an Arnold Schwarzenegger movie plastered to the wall in the station. A picture of the oversized actor was accompanied by a text—the gist of which was that a firefighter had lost his wife and child in a terrorist attack and was out for vengeance. It made me sick.

I was not alone. Immediately following the devastation in New York, Hollywood recanted. *The New York Times* carried articles in which studio powerhouses made dramatic statements about how everything had changed. A new era had dawned. A novelist and screenwriter declared on television that she would never write the same stories again. Sincerity charged back. Several periodicals pronounced "irony" dead. An acerbic, often cynical film reviewer for *The New Yorker* ended his column with a heartfelt statement about love. He seemed to mean it. My brother-in-law, a sculptor, reported a conversation that he had with fellow artists who said they were rethinking their work. For a brief time, photographs of firefighters and policemen replaced pictures of celebrities in the tabloids and on magazine covers. The news channels dropped commercials from their coverage, as if they knew that alternating film footage from the site, where rescue workers were digging for pieces of the dead, with ads for dishwashing liquid or an allergy drug would be unacceptable. But by now, this talk of a cultural sea change is mostly gone. *Collateral Damage*, the Schwarzenegger film, was withdrawn but later released, and now it has come and gone. The movie moguls backed away from their statements, arguing that they had been in shock and didn't know what they were saying. Television commercials were reinstated long ago, and images of corpses lying in the fields or cities of other countries are cut short by pleas to rush into your nearest Ford dealer to save hundreds of dollars on a new SUV. As for irony, the word had been misused so often in the press before September 11, had been trumpeted far and wide as the tone of our age, as if it meant nothing more than a cold and cynical distance. Irony is always double. The juxtaposition between the declarations made immediately after 9/11 in the media, announcing a new earnest world, and the return to business as usual only months afterward might serve as a singular proof that the ironic point of view is sometimes the only legitimate way to interpret the reality we live in.

3

There aren't so many flags in the city now. Some still hang outside houses or flutter from the radio antennae of cars and taxis, but they are no longer ubiquitous. In the city, we understood those flags, but many Europeans I have spoken to in these past months mistook them for American chauvinism. They weren't. They were what we had—a sign of solidarity— and they appeared spontaneously on that day in September. Who knew that so many people had old flags in their closets? On the Friday after the attacks, twenty thousand people from my neighborhood streamed onto Seventh Avenue with candles to honor the dead firefighters from our Park Slope station. Many people carried flags or wore flags or had dressed themselves in red, white, and blue. There are a lot of old hippies in our neighborhood. During elections, 98 percent of us vote for Democrats. Many of us, including me and my husband, marched against the Vietnam War. That night someone in the crowd began singing "We Shall Overcome," the old protest song from the civil rights movement that carried on into the anti-war movement. The last thing anybody in that crowd wanted was more blood. The United States is still at war, and if New Yorkers were jingoists, the flags would still be omnipresent—and their meaning would have changed.

4

"Everybody was *so nice* after September 11, you remember that?" one woman said to another on the subway a couple of months ago. She had a loud voice, a heavy Russian accent, and while she hung onto a pole with one hand, she gestured emphatically with the other. Her companion spoke softly, and I heard in her sentence the lilt of the islands, Trinidad or St. Lucia, perhaps. "It's back to the old ways now," she agreed. It's true. We were wonderful during the crisis, and we were tender to one another. Volunteers streamed to the site. After only a few days there were so many, they were turned away by the hundreds. Our local bookstore became a donation center and was so overwhelmed by garbage bags, flashlights, boots, socks, and gloves that the owner posted polite but firm signs that made it clear she couldn't accept any more supplies. Here in Brooklyn, block after block organized bake, tag, and book sales to raise money for the families of the dead. Strangers spoke to each other in the street, in stores, and on the subway. That need to ask, to tell, is over now. People have returned to the business of living their private lives.

Those of us who are not widows, widowers, or the children of a dead parent have moved from active grief to the repression necessary for recovery, a state of mind that is possible only because the city hasn't been attacked again and, unlike people in some parts of the world, we are not occupied or living under daily siege. The impromptu memorials of candles and teddy bears, poems and letters, have disappeared. Nobody has mentioned gas masks, Cipro, escape ladders, or kayaks to me for a long time. There was a run on kayaks in the city, purchased by anxious citizens who intended to drop the slender boats into the rivers and paddle upstate or to New Jersey when the next target blew. The fires have finally stopped burning at the site, and the city is no longer counting and recounting its dead.

P.S. 234 was closed for four months. The children returned to school in January, and Juliette was glad to be back. One of her classmates, a girl who would not let go of her mother for weeks after the attacks, who clung to the maternal body wherever it was—on the toilet, in the bathtub, or asleep in bed—is once again a freewheeling second-grader. The three-year-old boy who refused to walk, telling his parents he didn't want his feet to touch the ground because he was afraid of "burning sticks," no longer needs to be carried everywhere. The police roadblocks below Canal Street are gone, and now hundreds of visitors to the city stand in line to buy tickets to view the site of the devastation. The gaping hole in the ground has become New York's number one tourist attraction. I know of only one family in my neighborhood that sold their house after the attacks and moved to the suburbs. Connecticut is an unlikely target. For months afterward everyone was worried about the air downtown. Nobody could say what was in it. Crossing the Brooklyn Bridge in a cab, I still sometimes imagine a sudden explosion, steel and concrete giving way beneath the vehicle and my own sad, sudden death in the East River. But like a lot of people in the city, I'm a fatalist or, as my mother used to say, "philosophical."

The truth is I can't leave New York because I'm mad about it, hopelessly in love with this place in a way that is usually reserved for a person. And in this, too, I'm not alone. It's a big, bad, wonderful city—loud, raucous, and nasty—but it's also kind and dear. I've lived here for twenty-four years, and I'm not over my love affair yet. There are parts of this city so ugly,

I find them gorgeous. I've always been attached to the litter, the graffiti, to the noisy, jolting trains, and it seems that despite my antipathy to them, I'm rather attached to surly garbagemen, mute cabdrivers, and overly charming waiters as well. There was a hush in New York for a while—an eerie calm that attends the rites of mourning. You still feel it near Ground Zero, but away from the site, people have been sniping at each other again for months. They're yelling at meter maids. Truck drivers are howling obscenities at jaywalking pedestrians, and straphangers are shoving each other in the subway. But, just as before, people rush to help a person who's fallen on the sidewalk. They dole out loose change to bums and con artists and musicians and troops of young boys who sing in harmony on the trains. And New Yorkers of both sexes and all classes still send you compliments or encouragement on the fly—"Love your hat, honey," "Great coat," or, "Hey there, slim, give us a smile."

5

One day in March, my husband was watching *42nd Street* on television—the 1933 film musical. Near the end, Ruby Keeler appears in a blouse and a small pair of shorts. She swings her arms and her feet start to tap like crazy—shuffling, sliding, and hitting her marks on the stage as if there's no tomorrow. As Paul sat on the sofa and watched the gutsy dancer, at once tough and feminine, he felt tears come to his eyes, and he gave way to a moment of hopeless sentimentality. "For the old New York," he told me, "not for September 10, but for what used to be." Paul was born in 1947. In 1933, he was nobody, but the fact is that New York is as much a myth as a place, and because we all participate in that fiction, we make it partly real. After September 11, the imaginary New York of the century now gone—the wisecracking, rough-and-tumble world of gangsters and dolls, of cigarette girls in absurd outfits, of the Cotton Club, of hot jazz, of hipsters and Beats, of low-lying clubs dense with smoke or Abstract Expressionists at fisticuffs in the Cedar Bar—have become more poignant to us than ever.

The inhabitants of this city have always known that the rest of the country doesn't like us much, that New York inspires fear, anger, and irritation in middle America. I know. I grew up there. We had our moment in the sun. For a few months, we looked awfully good to other parts of the United States, but not a single person I spoke to in the city thought it would last, and it hasn't. We're not all that loved from the outside, so we love ourselves fiercely, and we perpetuate and celebrate our own myths—the poems and books and plays and movies and all those songs about our greatness—and the terrible wound inflicted on this town has only made a good number of us more fervent.

6

Real New York and imaginary New York aren't easily separated. The stuff of a city isn't only material; it's spiritual as well. What is true is that 40 percent of us are now foreign-born. A few years ago, I read in the newspaper that in a single elementary school in Queens, the children spoke sixty-four different languages at home. Riding the subway, I routinely see people reading newspapers in Spanish, Russian, Polish, Chinese, Arabic, and other languages I'm too ignorant to identify. New Yorkers aren't bound by a common tongue or by similar backgrounds. We're everybody from everywhere, and most of the time, we tolerate each other pretty well. The people in this city know that in this we are unique. No other place comes close to our diversity. We have our share of ugliness, brutality, and pockets of cruel and stupid racism, but the fact is that if you don't like the hectic jostling of innumerable cultures and languages and ways of being, you wouldn't want to live here. The terrorists understood nothing. When they hurt New York, they hurt the whole world.

These days New Yorkers are talking about September 11, 2002, and how we will get through it. It isn't only that people fear another attack on the city, but that the date itself will force us to relive a trauma, which, despite our efforts to live normally, is still raw and undigested. My sister Asti told me that she dreads the approaching anniversary so intensely that she tries not to think about it. A journalist friend of mine, who's traveled the world reporting from some of the most dangerous war zones for National Public Radio, is hosting a program on that day. She said that for the first time she's worried about breaking down and crying on the air. What the Memorial should look like and what should be built downtown have become hotly contested issues. More and more people are saying that they want the towers back. I understand how they feel. For a year now, looking at the skyline has hurt me. We all got used to those two enormous and, frankly, rather ugly pillars that loomed above us. But the dead can't be brought back to life, and even if the city were to rebuild exact replicas of the fallen structures, they could never be more than twin ghosts of a city we can never reclaim. It is better to face their absence as our painful collective scar and to celebrate and protect what has not changed about New York—the city of immigrants, of pluralism, and of tolerance.

Nobody who was here in the city will forget that day of mass murder, and as the first anniversary comes nearer, I recognize that for most of us the ugly memory surges back at the slightest prompting, and for each one of us, the memory is different. Some saw arms and legs falling from the sky. Some waited for a phone call that never came. Some ran for their lives. Some stood frozen on the street in disbelief. Some wandered in Brooklyn with face masks as the debris blew across the borough. Some in the Bronx and Queens saw only the blue sky turn black with smoke.

Both in the United States and around the world, *9/11* has become a media euphemism batted around in political debates from both the right and the left with a glibness and ease that's rather frightening. But it seems to me that like other crimes committed against human beings around the world in the name of varying ideologies and religions, the attacks on the World Trade Center can only be understood through individual people, because if we lose sight of the particular—of one man's or one woman's or one child's suffering and loss— we risk losing sight of our common humanity, and that is a form of blindness, not only to others but to ourselves.

2002

The Bostonians: Personal and Impersonal Words

"IT IS NOT THAT I HAVE ANYTHING STRANGE OR NEW TO RE-late," the twenty-eight-year-old Henry James wrote to Charles Eliot Norton in 1872. "In fact when one sits down to sum up Cambridge life *plume en main*, the strange thing seems its aridity." In 1913, two weeks before his seventieth birthday, James would use the same word, this time as an adjective, to describe the city in which his family had settled in Massachusetts. By then he had been living in England for many years, and in a letter to his sister-in-law, Alice, he declared a visit to America impossible. He could not, he explained, spend the summer in "utterly arid and vacuous Cambridge." I am interested in this repetition because, despite the image of desiccation, twelve years after the first letter and twenty-nine years before the second, Henry James devoted an entire novel to that *arid* part of the world and called it *The Bostonians*.

Although Henry James, Jr., was born in New York City and spent a good part of his childhood en route from one European city to another, as he, his siblings, and their mother followed the restless Continental wanderings of Henry James,

Sr., Boston and Cambridge would become deeply familiar places for the novelist. During the academic year 1862–63, he studied law at Harvard before giving it up for a life of writing. His family moved to Boston in 1864 and shortly thereafter settled permanently in Cambridge at 20 Quincy Street. But long before the family's relocation, the ideas of New England had been running in Henry Senior's blood. The James children grew up in an atmosphere of idealism, reform, and new thought. Henry David Thoreau, Ralph Waldo Emerson, and other Transcendentalists, including Margaret Fuller, William Ellery Channing, and Bronson Alcott, were all friends of the family. Henry Senior was also an ardent advocate of immediate emancipation for the slaves, and he sent his two younger sons, Garth Wilkinson and Robertson, to the Concord Academy, where Thoreau had taught and where three of Emerson's children were enrolled, as was Nathaniel Hawthorne's son, Julian. Under the direction of the abolitionist Franklin Sanborn, a fund-raiser and active conspirator in John Brown's stand at Harpers Ferry, the school was more than an experiment in coeducation; it was a locus of feverish ideology. Both Wilkie and Bob left school to fight for the Union cause. Wilkie enlisted at seventeen and not long after joined the first regiment of black troops as adjutant to Colonel Robert Gould Shaw. On May 28, 1863, accompanied by rousing fanfare, the 54th marched out of Boston. By the end of July that same year, nearly half its men and most of its officers had been killed during the assault on Fort Wagner in Charleston Bay. Wilkie James was badly injured but survived. After the war, he and Robertson, subsidized by their father, became the owners of a plantation in Florida that employed black laborers. The venture failed, but their effort remains a testament not only to the idealism of the brothers but to the hopes of the world that played a crucial role in shaping them—zealous, high-minded New England.

There were other ideas wafting about the James household—imported ones. A disciple of both Emanuel Swedenborg, the Swedish natural scientist turned mystic, and François-Marie Charles Fourier, the French social philosopher, Henry Senior embraced a miasmic coupling of spiritual enlightenment (Swedenborg believed he had found a key to an angelic reading of the Scriptures) and a utopian vision of a new society in which human beings freed from repression and inhibition could release their true passionate selves and lead orderly, harmonious lives in communities known as phalanxes.

As in every age, rigorous intellectual ideas mingled with more dubious notions. In both Europe and the United States, a rage for Mesmerism and the occult shook fashionable society and intellectual circles. Séances abounded. The novelist's brother William James, the great American philosopher and psychologist, maintained a belief in spiritualism throughout his life and hoped to continue his researches beyond the grave. He asked his wife to try to contact him after he was dead, and she did try, but in vain. On another occasion, however, without his widow present, William was reported to have spoken from the other side. When Henry received news of the phantom voice, he called it "the most abject and impudent, the hollowest, vulgarest, and basest rubbish." Then, as now, vegetarianism was in vogue among the forward thinking, but the enlightened fell for other health fads as well. A number of the Transcendentalists became enamored of Fletcherism, an eating practice that encouraged chewing food into a liquid mush before swallowing. Henry Junior took up the cause for a while and masticated with such vigor that William, a nonbeliever, blamed Fletcherism for Henry's myriad bowel troubles.

If contemporary readers find these beliefs and ideas remote, I ask them to pause and reconsider. We live in an age of religious sects and mad militias, of gurus scattered about the country from California to New York, an age of channeling, colonics, crystals, and raw food crazes. In the United States, utopian quests for purity, perfection, and self-improvement, no matter how wacky, have always found fertile ground in which to flourish. The question remains, however: Why did Henry James describe the lively intellectual climate (with its admittedly nutty fringes) of Boston and its environs as "arid" and "vacuous"? James felt that American culture was simply too young and too thin to sustain him as an artist. He was continually pulled by the lure of Europe, by its old and visible history—its architecture, painting, ruins, and, of course, its literature.

For James, the single most important American writer was Nathaniel Hawthorne. He read and loved Hawthorne's books as a youth, and although the young writer never met his literary mentor, the spiritual connection between the two writers would never be dissolved. Hawthorne, a sublime storyteller who criticized both American Puritanism and utopianism in his fiction, became *the* American literary precedent for James. When he woke up on May 19, 1864, to the news that the great American novelist was dead, the young Henry James sat on his bed and wept. Like most literary sons, however, he was critical of the father, and when writing about Hawthorne he articulates his ambivalence about American fiction:

But our author must accept the awkward as well as the graceful side of his fame; for he has the advantage of pointing a valuable moral. This moral is that the flower of art blooms only where the soil is deep, that it takes a great deal of history to produce a little literature, that it needs a complex social machinery to set a writer in motion. American civilization has hitherto had other things to do than produce flowers, and before giving birth to writers it has widely occupied itself with providing something for them to write about. Three or four beautiful talents of transatlantic growth are the sum of what the world usually recognizes, and in this modest nosegay the genius of Hawthorne is admitted to have the rarest and sweetest fragrance.

However shallow James may have found American literary soil, he acknowledged that Hawthorne sprouted from it, and *The Bostonians* owes a debt to the older writer's work, *The Blithedale Romance* in particular, which was inspired by Hawthorne's brief discontented stay at Brook Farm: Margaret Fuller's Transcendentalist-Fourierist experiment in communal living. In his essay "Brook Farm and Concord," James quotes the words of the skeptic, Coverdale, from Hawthorne's utopian romance: "No sagacious man will long retain his sagacity if he live exclusively among reformers and progressive people, without periodically returning to the settled system of things, to correct himself by a new observation from the old standpoint." It is a sentence that speaks directly to *The Bostonians*, not to any particular character but to the effect of the narrative as a whole, which unearths its truths through the continual push and pull of people and ideas that find themselves in rigid opposition.

In the novel, two ideologies and two people are pitted against one another. In its simplest terms, the book presents us with a conflict between a reformer and a reactionary, between a triumphant North and a defeated South, between a woman and a man. *The Bostonians* is a novel of ideas, but the ideas articulated by James's two battling characters, who are also distant cousins, Olive Chancellor, a Boston spinster and champion of women's rights, and Basil Ransom, a bitter arch-conservative from Mississippi, are not the ideas the book probes. Indeed, both characters are guilty of mouthing senti-mental or clichéd tripe, and I don't think their creator was ter-ribly interested in their beliefs per se. He was drawn by something infinitely more complex than a conflict between two hardened ideological positions. Like all of James's novels, *The Bostonians* is an investigation of what happens *between* and *among* people, and how that arena of interaction can take on a life of its own and determine the fates of those involved.

Miss Chancellor and Mr. Ransom are ferocious rivals in what becomes a love triangle. Both want possession of Verena Tarrant, the pretty, weak, and very charming product of a Cambridge quack healer and the daughter of an abolitionist. The innocent Verena, who has a "gift" for inspirational speak-ing, is nothing if not a child of the *new ideas*. "She had sat on the knees of somnambulists, and had been passed from hand to hand by trance speakers; she was familiar with every kind of 'cure' and had grown up among lady editors advocating new religions, and people who disapproved of the marriage-tie." Through this tug-of-war over a person, Verena, who is also the creature of a particular New England subculture, James explores the psychological implications of belief—how a climate of ideas can invade, affect, mingle with, and be used, both consciously and unconsciously, by a person in the throes of passion.

The book's intellectual vigor, then, is not located in what the characters *say* they believe, in their dogmatic positions, but rather in a dialectical tension between the "personal" and the "impersonal," the "private" and the "public," the "particular" and the "general." These words in their various forms occur so often in the novel that they become a conspicuous and pointed refrain. What they *mean*, however, is another, far more complicated problem. Because *The Bostonians* skips from one person's point of view to another's, the narrator gives us access to the thoughts of all his major characters and to each one's idiosyncratic uses of these words, a fact that further complicates their meaning. When Basil first meets his cousin Olive, he notes the bourgeois opulence of her house and feels that he has never found himself "in the presence of so much organized privacy." This is exactly the realm in which he hopes to place Verena. He emphatically believes that she is "meant for privacy, for him, for love." On the other hand, the narrator tells us that Mrs. Farrinder, formidable spokeswoman for the Emancipation of Women, has "something public in her eye, which was large, cold, and quiet . . ." The foggy, attenuated Miss Birdseye, relic of an earlier abolitionist age, is also a being of generalities, a person who, though rumored to have had a Hungarian lover in her youth, could never, the narrator tells us, "have entertained a sentiment so personal. She was in love, even in those days, only with causes." Dr. Prance, on the other hand, devoted physician and living proof of female competence in a profession usually reserved for men, has no use for causes: "She looked about her with a kind of near-sighted deprecation, and seemed to hope that she should not be expected to generalize in any way . . ." The society matron Mrs. Burrage, only marginally involved in causes, is also a woman whose "favours" are "general not particular." Selah Tarrant stresses that his daughter's success as a speaker is "thoroughly impersonal," and Verena herself insists that when she addresses an audience "it is not *me* . . ." In sharp contrast, Ransom, as he watches Verena's performance, thinks to himself that what he is witnessing is "an intensely personal exhibition." And while Olive Chancellor hopes and believes that she will never be like her frivolous sister, Mrs. Luna, who is "so personal, so narrow," Basil Ransom finds Olive to be "intensely, fearfully, a person." Verena, too, discovers "how peculiarly her friend" Olive is "constituted, how nervous and serious, how personal, how exclusive . . ." The words slip according to each character's perceptions, blind spots, and feelings, and only through their interplay can we begin to make sense of James's meaning.

In a letter to his friend Grace Norton, who was going through a difficult time in her life, James gave this advice: "Only don't I beseech you generalize too much in these sympathies and tendernesses—remember that every life is a special problem which is not yours but another's and content yourself with the terrible algebra of your own. Don't melt too much into the universe, but be as solid and dense and fixed as you can." On the other hand, when Hugh Walpole, novelist and friend of James, quoted "The Master" in his diary, the sentiment expressed appears to be quite different: "I've had one great passion in my life—the intellectual passion . . . Make it your rule to encourage the impersonal interest as against the personal—but remember also that they are interdependent." The two passages dramatize what I would call the focused ambiguity of James's language. He begged Grace not to "generalize" or "melt" but rather to encourage in herself the particular, the personal, the fixed, and he advised Hugh to encourage the opposite, "the impersonal interest," with the important caveat that he remember the impersonal and the personal are always connected.

The apparent contradiction reveals Jamesian semantics. In each case, he is speaking to a particular friend, and his imparted wisdom reflects his understanding of each person's psychological needs. James must have felt that Grace's abstract effusions needed taming. On the other hand, he was giving Hugh paternal literary advice. In the world of James, there are no absolutes, no final truths, no static realities. The solidity he urges on Grace Norton is only a relative one. Language, after all, is impersonal and personal, particular and general, both inside us and outside us, and James writes with a profound awareness of this fact. Words are where the public and private intersect. In *The Bostonians*, Henry James turns the public and private inside out, and the engines behind that reversal are external and internal—a particular cultural atmosphere and sexual passion.

In terms of setting, the novel moves away from the "organized privacy" of Olive's rooms at the beginning of the novel to a public building at its very end: Boston's Music Hall, where Verena is scheduled to speak and where the story reaches its piercing crescendo. In between are scenes that take place in private, semi-private, and semi-public places. The second environment is Miss Peabody's dim, drab, and "featureless" apartment, where Mrs. Farrinder is supposed to address a gathering of the sympathetic. The reader's introduction to Miss Birdseye (a character all of New England took as a swipe at Elizabeth Peabody, Sophia Hawthorne's sister and sister-in-law of the novelist) has a comic pathos that well illustrates the novel's worried strain between the general and the particular: "The long practice of philanthropy had not given accent to her features; it had rubbed out their transitions, their meanings. The waves of sympathy, of enthusiasm, had wrought upon them in the same way in which the waves of time finally modify the surface of old marble busts, gradually washing away their sharpness, their details." Even poor Miss Birdseye's face has become impersonal and unfocused, as empty and unfurnished as the rooms she occupies, an interior that causes the bourgeois Olive a pang and makes "her wonder whether an absence of nice arrangements were a necessary part of the enthusiasm for humanity." As the novel's most extreme altruist, Miss Peabody suffers from a loss of self.

The far more complex Olive Chancellor wishes with her whole being to emulate the selflessness of the aging abolitionist, to escape the pains, rigors, and tormented confinement of her own body. For Olive, however, the Emancipation of Women is far more than another good cause to support; it is a deeply personal echo of her own psychological and sexual imprisonment. Even before she lays eyes on Verena, the reader knows that Miss Chancellor has dreamed that she might "know intimately some *very* poor girl." The shopgirls she approaches, however, are wary and confused by her attentions, and inevitably mixed up with some young "Charlie," an impediment Olive comes to "dislike . . . extremely." Olive Chancellor is clearly in love, and her love for Verena conveys the hunger of sexual longing, but it would be a serious misreading of the novel to suppose either that Olive and Verena are "doing it" behind the scenes or that Olive has fully admitted to herself that the desperation she feels about Verena is connected to her desire for physical love.

Despite the fact that nineteenth-century mores, particularly in the United States, were far more repressive of homosexuality than those of our own time, there was nevertheless a greater tolerance and far less suspicion of intimate friendships between women that included physical signs of affection. The word *crush* was often used to describe the feelings of girls in school who fell for other girls, for example, and the term was used without the "taint" of homosexuality. Although relatively more open to same-sex unions, contemporary

American culture nevertheless bristles with a need to catego-
rize human eroticism, a force that by its very nature resists
definition and plays a role in most relations between people of
either and both sexes, whether it is acted upon or not. In
other words, when *The Bostonians* was published, James's les-
bian portraits were subject to greater ambiguity than they are
now, and in certain passages James plays on the vagaries of
sexual identity, the shifting, indefinable motion between the
masculine and the feminine: "It was true that if she had been
a boy she would have borne some relation to a girl, whereas
Doctor Prance appeared to bear none whatever." In hot pursuit of Verena Tarrant, Basil Ransom fantasizes an end to her
involvement with the cause: ". . . but in the presence of a man
she should really care for, this false, flimsy structure would
rattle to her feet, and the emancipation of Olive Chancellor's
sex (what sex was it, great heaven? he used profanely to ask
himself) would be relegated to the land of vapours, of dead
phrases."

But Ransom has misunderstood the power of "vapours"
and "dead phrases," which play a transforming role in the
novel, both in public and in private. Like a contagious fog
over a city, these enunciations, no matter how hackneyed, are
invested with the power to seduce and cast a spell over an
audience—be it hundreds of people or just one. The dead
phrases of both sides—the reactionary utterances of Mr. Ransom and the radical declarations of Boston's feminists—are
animated by the human voice, to which the story assigns an
almost magical power. For the bulk of the narrative, the most
compelling voice belongs to Verena. She is the enchantress
whose speeches hold her listeners "under the charm," as she
delivers addresses that are more akin to musical performance
than lecture. Like a sorceress in a fairy tale, Verena is "spin-

ning vocal sounds to a silver thread." She also entrances Ransom. When he seeks her out in Cambridge, he understands that he is falling in love with her, and his vision of her is marked by the heightened brilliance that illuminates a beloved. He compares her to a nymph, and she makes him think of "unworldly places." Olive similarly imagines that her new friend's wonderful qualities have "dropped straight from heaven, without filtering through her parents." Verena Tarrant shines, but the source of that luminosity, her bewitching hold over audiences, over Basil Ransom and over Olive Chancellor, is connected less to the presence of particular qualities in her personality than to their absence. The girl lacks self-consciousness and, like Miss Peabody, she has no grounded, no defined self. When she repeats to Ransom a phrase she has spoken twice before during the course of the novel, "Oh, it isn't me, you know. It's something outside!" she is both repeating what her prompters have told her and telling a truth about herself. James is getting at something I have always felt—that the public person inevitably slides into the third person, away from *I* and into *he* or *she*. *The Bostonians* explores an early incarnation of what will eventually become American celebrity culture. James saw it coming, and the novel anticipates the moment when human beings would be emptied of all inner human qualities and turned into images, commodities to be bought and sold on the open market for profit, a time when celebrities would fall into the curious but fitting habit of referring to themselves in the third person.

Before movies, radio, and television, publicity meant newspapers. In terms of the narrative, it is apt that Verena has sprung from a paternal seed that has no individual, no private character. Selah Tarrant isn't only a humbug; he is a humbug obsessed with the idea of public recognition and the money to be made from it. Like a shuddering moth near a lamp, Terrant is irresistibly drawn to the glare of publicity. He haunts newspaper offices and printing rooms, hoping against hope that he will somehow be noticed. The most fervent wish of Selah Tarrant's tawdry, corrupt little heart is to be interviewed by some newspaperman. There is an active journalist in *The Bostonians,* someone whose very name is an apology—Mathias Pardon. He hovers at the edges of the story throughout, showing up first at Miss Peabody's and finally at the Music Hall, with appearances in between. An embodiment of the unconscious smarminess of the press, Pardon has scruples only in his patronymic. He is wholly unaware that his questions might be indelicate or intrusive, and he plows merrily ahead with his vapid articles. Although Pardon is a comic character, his vulgarity has sinister undertones; the man is morally vacant. "His faith, again, was the faith of Selah Tarrant—that being in the newspapers is a condition of bliss, and that it would be fastidious to question the terms of that privilege." It is hard to read this sentence without feeling its prescience. It is a faith that would eventually lead to the grotesque national spectacle of contemporary American life in which countless people humiliate and debase themselves in public for the dubious glory of being "on TV."

The paradox of publicity is that it enacts a reversal between the private and public. The press, especially the part of the press that reports on culture, continually converts what is meant for public consumption—art—into mere gossip about people's private lives: "For this ingenuous son of the age [Pardon] all distinction between the person and the artist had ceased to exist; the writer was personal, the person food for the newsboys, and everything and every one were every one's business." Pardon lurks on the sidelines of Verena's rise to stardom, hungry to scoop the story. The afternoon before the event at the Music Hall, the journalist searches high and low for Olive and Verena without success and finally insinuates himself into the family house, where he hammers Olive's sister with demands for "any little personal items" she might provide about either the speaker or her coach. The public, Pardon says, is almost as interested in Miss Chancellor as in Miss Tarrant. Under the banner of *the public* and *publicity*, the grand cause to emancipate women, a cause Olive champions as a force for "human progress," is transformed into vulgar prattle about domestic arrangements.

Although both Basil and Olive regard Verena as an otherworldly presence, she is decidedly not. Verena has lived her entire young life on the public stage, a life that has robbed her of all inner fixity, all knowledge of her own desires, and it is precisely this floating, externalized quality that makes her exceedingly vulnerable. The girl who can sway the great public will be brutally manipulated in her private life. It is to James's great credit that a malleable character like Verena, a person who is rather like an empty vessel filled over time with the "dead phrases" of others—first her father's, then Olive's, and finally Basil's—is nevertheless a fully believable human being. Her friendship with and loyalty to Olive Chancellor, her attraction to Basil Ransom, and her sweet, confused desire to please them both has all the poignancy of a child trapped in a custody battle. Verena's dawning awareness that she has an inner life and personal desires turns on a secret she keeps from Olive. She does not tell her friend that she has seen Basil Ransom in Cambridge. This, the narrator writes, is "the only secret she had in the world—the only thing that was all her own." Understandably, she is reluctant to give it up.

There is nothing more private than a secret, and a secret is of course silent. Silence belongs to solitude, the voice to the outside world. Unlike the voluble Verena, Olive is afflicted by silence. Nervous in the extreme, she sometimes finds herself dumbstruck and must struggle through her fits of muteness before she can find her voice. Despite a passionate desire to speak in public, she suffers from a nature so private it has become a debility. There is an aspect of the ventriloquist in James's spinster. She speaks through Verena, finds her voice in another body. It is Olive, Verena tells Ransom, who writes the speeches: "She tells me what to say—the real things, the strong things. It's Miss Chancellor as much as me!" This is intimate territory, the occupation of one person by another, and there is violence in it—the grasping, feverish desire not only to commingle with the beloved but to take total possession of her. Words assume the place of sexual penetration in *The Bostonians*. Words enter Verena, and words cause her destruction. The most powerful words, however, belong not to Olive Chancellor but to Basil Ransom.

Like Olive, Basil longs to find a public forum where his ideas might be heard. His effort is stymied, not by pathological shyness but by the simple fact that his ideas are too unpopular, at least in the North, to find much of an audience. Although he has written several essays and submitted them to publishers, they have been turned down. The narrator informs us that in one of these rejection letters an editor suggested to Ransom that three hundred years earlier he might easily have found a journal willing to print his thoughts. He has simply come too late. As an unpublished author, Ransom is rendered voiceless in the public sphere where he longs to speak. His frustration mirrors Olive's, and his motives for chasing Verena are equally intricate, despite the fact that his end desire is the opposite of Olive's. He wants to render Verena mute in public. To borrow the words of Mrs. Burrage, he intends to "shut her up altogether." We know Ransom has elaborate arguments for this position and that, like his feminist opponent, he is sincere. Neither Mr. Ransom nor Miss Chancellor is guilty of cant, but the Mississippian is also the indigent but proud survivor of a ruined South, where his mother and sisters still live in the penurious circumstances of defeat. Olive, too, lost her only two brothers in the war (an echo of James's soldier siblings), but despite their deaths, as a Northerner, she didn't lose a way of life. Ransom's family lost everything but its gentility, and early in the novel, as he sits in Olive Chancellor's parlor and waits for her to make her first appearance, the reader is introduced to the tinge of resentment that colors his experience: "He ground his teeth a little as he thought of the contrasts of the human lot; this cushioned feminine nest made him feel unhoused and underfed." Ransom is a man whose every move and word is affected by the memory of suffering, and like Olive he has clutched at ideas that reflect his feelings of personal injury and an unrecognized, but nevertheless evident, hunger for vengeance.

Once Ransom's attraction to Verena has become conscious love, his pursuit of her is increasingly described in terms of force. "In playing with the subject this way, in enjoying her visible hesitation, he was slightly conscious of a man's brutality—of being pushed by an impulse to test her good nature, which seemed to have no limit." Later he understands that his relentless pressure has made her "tremendously open to attack . . . ," that he is engaged in a "siege." By the end of the novel, Verena is in a state of "surrender" and he has "by muscular force, wrenched her away . . ." from Olive and the waiting public. The war imagery is obvious. James is pointing to a second, far more personal version of the North/South conflict, but Mr. Ransom's victory over Miss Chancellor, his conquest of Verena and her future in domestic bondage, isn't achieved by "muscular force" but by talk.

It is interesting to note that Ransom's decision to chase Verena in earnest, despite his poverty and dim prospects, is fueled by the rather flimsy justification that one of his essays has at last found a publisher. A single publication does not change Ransom's financial future, but he seizes upon it as a sign of a new public voice, which invigorates him in his quest to silence Verena's. The newly acquired stature as public speaker gives credence to Ransom's private utterance, a marriage proposal, just as his anti-feminist ideas justify his very *personal* advance on Verena. The eloquent phrases describing the pathos of female oppression, which Olive feeds to Verena, can't contend with Basil's verbal seduction. His most potent phrase turns out to be his accusation that Miss Tarrant isn't real. He tells her that in her desire to please others she has come to resemble "a preposterous little puppet" commandeered from behind the scenes, and the suitor turns his love object's own phrase against her: "It isn't *you*; the least in the world." What she originally believed was selfless devotion to a cause, a belief that allowed her to proclaim with pride, "It isn't me," is transformed through Ransom's steady rhetorical assault into an accusation of fraud: ". . . these words, the most effective and penetrating he had uttered, had sunk into her soul and worked and fermented there. She had come at last to believe them and that was the alteration, the transformation." Sentence by sentence, Ransom enters the inner sanctum of her doubts. Although he has touched on a truth and offers Verena the hope of "standing forth in . . . freedom," his is finally a promise of continued captivity under another name. Verena's fate is sad, but she is too wobbly and empty a character to be tragic, and Basil Ransom's hunger for Verena Tarrant is augmented by the stature of his adversary, Olive Chancellor, who, unlike Verena, is truly his equal. In terms of the book's politics, this irony creates a final and terrible resonance. It also redeems James from the charge that *The Bostonians* is somehow against women. It is a book uncomfortable with causes but deeply, intimately comfortable with women.

In the novel, only Olive Chancellor achieves tragic dimensions, and it is because of all the characters in the book she feels most, and feeling is the domain where Henry James is transcendent. The painfully private Olive Chancellor will in the end suffer the horror of public exposure and failure as well as the loss of the person whom she loves most passionately in the world, and it is a fate she has brought upon herself. Her culpability, however, doesn't in the least diminish the depth or reality of her pain or this reader's immense pity for her. Stiff, humorless, prejudiced, and half-blind to the reasons for her actions, the little Boston spinster becomes in her profound sorrow and humiliation heroic.

> . . . as soon as Ransom looked at her he became aware that the weakness she had just shown had passed away. She had straightened herself again, and she was upright in her desolation. The expression of her face was a thing to remain with him forever; it was impossible to imagine a more vivid presentment of blighted hope and wounded pride. Dry, desperate rigid, she yet wavered and seemed uncertain; her pale glittering eyes straining forward, as if they were looking for death. Ransom had a vision, even at that crowded moment, that if she could have met it there and then, bristling with steel or lurid with fire, she would have rushed on it without a tremor, like the heroine that she was.

"In the arts," James wrote, "feeling is always meaning." For me, these words illuminate not only the novelist's *ars poetica* but also James's great strength as a writer. His experience of the world and his empathy for other people produced a body of work that adamantly refused ready categories, received ideas, and preordained notions of all kinds in favor of the difficult, strange, tender, and always multifarious arena of human relations and emotions. I think James felt that every attempt to reduce life to a system of beliefs—religious, political, or philosophical—must inevitably become a form of lying.

Late in his life, he tried to explain his wariness of systems to two politically engaged writers: George Bernard Shaw and H. G. Wells. As a member of the committee that had rejected a play by James, Shaw told its author in a letter, "People don't want works of art from you. They want help, they want above all encouragement." In his response, James argued: ". . . all direct 'encouragement'—the thing you enjoin me on—encouragement of the short cut and say 'artless' order, is really more likely than not to be shallow and misleading . . ." Wells had hurt James by publishing a cruel attack on the older writer in a satirical book called *Boon, The Mind of the Race*, in which he had, among other things, criticized his "view of life and literature." To Wells, James wrote, "I *have* no view of life and literature, I maintain, other than that our form of the latter in especial is admirable exactly by its range and variety, its plasticity and liberality, its fairly living on the sincere and shifting experience of the individual practitioner." And later in the letter, he elaborated further, "It is art that *makes* life, makes interest, makes importance, for our consideration and application of these things, and I know of no substitute whatever for the force and beauty of its process."

James believed in the power of art, not because he thought it would change the world or because he imagined it could be a mirror of life. Art, he explains to Wells, is "for the extension of life, which is the novel's best gift."

James was probably too subtle for his correspondents, but the idea of "extension" makes sense to me because art and the world can't be as easily divided as we sometimes imagine. One comes from the other, and they intermingle in the consciousness we as readers meet on the page. Art can and does make life, as James says, because when we encounter a great work of art it creates feeling, and that feeling in the reader, the viewer, or the listener is finally what the work *means*. I have lived with James's characters and stories for many years, and they do not leave me. They have become part of who I am, and I can't help but feel that their creator, who worried over his paltry sales and lack of popularity with the reading public, would have been very happy to know how I feel. He would have been glad to know that his work has lasted and grown in importance and that I am only one of many people who have been permanently altered by his books.

In its range and variety, its plasticity and liberality, *The Bostonians* is an embodiment of James's nonprescriptive idea about what a novel should be. Through a story that delineates the power of words to obfuscate, exploit, and distort human reality, Henry James offers his own nuanced, precise, and sensitive prose in opposition to the dead phrases that stream from lecture halls, line the pages of newspapers, and float from one speaker to another in that arid climate that was Boston. That city has changed and the United States has changed since James wrote his American novel, but dead phrases, empty rhetoric, clichéd thought, as well as ready-made opinions and just plain nonsense proffered to the public by the press show no sign of abating anytime soon.

I believe it's impossible to read *The Bostonians* without at least wondering about the ways we use language or language uses us. Moribund and idiotic political statements continue to influence and sway us because of the manner in which they are spoken or written. Even the most sincere declaration of devotion to a noble cause may be born from private venom or personal misery. There is always a gap between what we feel and what we say. Henry James knew that it was heartbreakingly difficult to capture the flux of experience in words, to articulate the riddle of human feelings and actions, but this was precisely his ambition, and I, as one of his faithful readers, love him for it.

2004

Charles Dickens and the
Morbid Fragment

"WHENEVER I AM AT PARIS, I AM DRAGGED BY SOME INVISIBLE force into the Morgue. I do not want to go there, but I am always pulled there." Charles Dickens gave this sentence to his narrator in *The Uncommercial Traveller*, but he used the same words to describe his own compulsion to look at dead bodies: "I am dragged by invisible force to the morgue." In 1847, this unseen power lured Dickens again and again to the Paris morgue, and on one of those visits he found himself enthralled by the disfigured, bloated body of a man who had been drowned. Sixteen years later, Dickens would begin a novel about drowning, *Our Mutual Friend*. It was to be the last book he finished before he died. The image of that nameless dead man lying on a slab in the morgue must have stayed with Dickens over the years like a ghost waiting for a story. The tale he came to write attacks the problem of the corpse with a full arsenal of verbal weaponry—humor, irony, and pathos. The dead body was Dickens's muse, the catalyst that generated the writing of *Our Mutual Friend*, the abject thing that launched a torrent of words to do battle with the truth every person faces: The corpse is my future. I will die.

The closer I find myself to death, the more threatening it becomes. The time I saw an open wound on an operating table, I fainted. A few years ago, I was in a car accident. Right after the crash, my vision blurred, I was overcome with nausea, and although I managed to retain consciousness, I went into shock. Even after I had been released from the hospital and sent home with the knowledge that I was only banged and bruised, I woke up with a start for several nights in a row to the impact—the sudden terrific blow that shattered the windshield and crushed the car around me. I felt it in my body as if it were happening again exactly as it had happened, and in my terror I was jolted awake. This dream image had no relation to other dreams I've had; it was brief and isolated—a reenactment of the moment the van hit us. I suspect that this "dream" was closer to traumatic memory. Soldiers in wars and victims of crimes or disasters may suffer from these unwanted memories for years—gruesome fragments of experiences that can't be digested because they don't make sense. The mind resists categorizing horror—it doesn't know where to put it—but traces of the incomprehensible may linger nevertheless; no longer fully conscious, they seem to float outside of place and time.

Dickens's traveler is drawn to view a body in the morgue, and then after he has seen it, he begins to imagine it everywhere. He goes to the baths and has a fantasy of the "large dark body" bobbing toward him. When he accidentally gulps down some bathwater, he recoils, thinking he senses "the contamination of the creature in it." Still later, "that very day, at dinner, some morsel on my plate looked like a piece of him." Although the body the traveler saw in the morgue was whole, he is haunted by a corpse that is both leaking and falling apart, a loathsome object that threatens to enter him as bacteria or food. His repulsion comes from an anxiety that the protective barrier between him and it will shift, fall, or crumble. Horror movies play on this fear all the time—that the dead are, well, not dead but moving about in the world, usually chasing some howling young woman. Although fantastic, these films don't lie. Eventually, death catches up with all of us.

Early in *Our Mutual Friend*, the reader encounters the first of several drowned bodies. A police inspector has taken charge of the corpse, but he has trouble knowing how to refer to the thing in his custody. He first addresses the dead man as "you"; then a little later, he announces to a bystander, "I still call it *him*, you see." Mr. Inspector is the first of a number of characters to have pronoun difficulties. What does it mean to call someone *you* or *him*? When does *he* turn into *it*? These are ultimate questions, and they are posed relentlessly in the novel. When I defended the dissertation I wrote on Dickens at Columbia University in 1986, Steven Marcus, the Dickens scholar and author of *From Pickwick to Dombey*, asked me if I thought Dickens *knew* what he was doing, if he knew that his work was metaphysical. I said, "No," and he agreed with me. But in art, knowing isn't everything—the unknown often pushes its way to the surface. In recent years, neuroscience has demonstrated that Freud was surely right in this sense: A huge part of what the brain does is unconscious. And every novelist can tell you that while writing, things happen. You don't know why the characters or their words appear to you or where they come from, but there they are, and often these peculiar ghosts and their voices, rising up from nowhere, are exactly the ones that are most crucial to the story.

The novel's plot turns on the identity of the drowned man Mr. Inspector calls "you," "him," and "it." This body is hauled from the Thames by Gaffer Hexam and his daughter, Lizzie, who then hand the corpse over to the authorities. The papers found on the body lead them to identify it as John Harmon, son of a London dust mogul and heir to a fortune. With the son dead, the money goes to the Boffins, The Golden Dustman and his wife, formerly loyal servants to Old Harmon. Silas Wegg, a sly observer of the Boffinses' new wealth, plots against them. A cash reward, offered for information leading to the perpetrator of the crime, inspires Rogue Riderhood, a low-life river rat, to a deception that takes him to the offices of Eugene Wrayburn and Mortimer Lightwood, lawyers for the Harmon estate. Riderhood then falsely accuses Gaffer Hexam, the man in the boat who found the body, of murder. This brings the highborn Eugene Wrayburn and the lowborn Lizzie Hexam together, and their love story begins. But the authorities are wrong. The body found in the river did not belong to John Harmon but to George Radfoot, a friend of Harmon's who bore a resemblance to the heir. This mistake allows John Harmon, who has been away from home for many years, to pose as someone else and become a spectator of his own death. He changes his name to Rokesmith, goes to live in what was once his father's house, works as a secretary to Boffin, and there observes the beautiful but spoiled Bella Wilfer, ward to the newly flush servants and the woman to whom he has been given in his father's will—his marriage to her being a condition of his inheritance—and their rocky courtship begins. Through social connection or simple coincidence all the dispersed elements of the story intersect: Lizzie and Bella meet. Bradley Headstone, schoolmaster to Lizzie's brother, and Eugene Wrayburn are thrown together and become rivals for Lizzie. In the grip of a terrible and fatal passion for Lizzie, Headstone allies himself with Riderhood.

Mayhem ensues. Riderhood, Headstone, and Gaffer all drown. Eugene Wrayburn almost drowns, but in the end couples are united, the wicked are punished, and most of the good characters seem headed for the fairy-tale state known as "happily ever after."

Seeing Things

Metaphor always changes the way we see things in our minds. When one thing is compared to another in a sentence, I merge the two in the mental picture I create while I'm reading. Dickens's metaphors, however, are more radical than those of most writers because they dismantle the lines of conventional perception, and I am continually reorienting the images I see in my mind as I read his books. Normal vision is determined to a large degree by our expectations. We learn to distinguish things as isolated identities *out there* through the way our brains develop to order visual and linguistic material that make "whole object" representations possible. To put it simply, we don't see a naked world but a visual field that has been determined by experience, memory, and language. Every reader of Dickens notices that in his work objects often have human traits and people often resemble things. This mixing of the inanimate and the animate is both funny and subversive. When Fascination Fledgeby wants to gain entrance to a house, for example, the reader is told, "he pulled the house's nose again and pulled and pulled . . . until a human nose appeared in the doorway." When the metaphorical nose is followed by a literal nose, the comic tension it creates undermines the status of both noses, making the "real" one appear alien and disembodied, as if it were floating alone in the dark space of a doorway. Dickens's language plays havoc with whole object representations by breaking them down. Rather than isolate the human body from its environment and make neat distinctions between the living and the nonliving, Dickens confuses these "normal" separations until, over time, he rearranges our expectations entirely.

In Silas Wegg, Dickens creates a character who is already *literally* part object. He has a wooden leg, which the narrator tells us Wegg seems "to have taken to naturally," perhaps because the man is also *metaphorically* wooden: "Wegg was a knotty man, and a close grained, with a face carved out of very hard material, that had just as much play of expression as a watchman's rattle." Both his body and facial tics are more thing-like than human. Then, in a chapter titled "Mr. Wegg Looks After Himself," we discover that the wooden gentleman has been reluctant to give up what he has lost, and obeying a wonderful logic all his own, he goes to a dingy little shop in London and calls on *himself*:

"And how have I been going on, this long time, Mr. Venus?"
"Very bad," says Mr. Venus, uncompromisingly.
"What am I still at home?" asks Wegg with an air of surprise.
"Always at home."

The first time I read this passage, I had no idea what was going on, but when it became clear to me that the "I" in this remarkable exchange is Wegg's lost leg bone, I burst out laughing. In order to arrive at this "I," Wegg has to wrench the familiar pronoun from its usual place and force it into another: He adopts what is normally the third person as the first. The French linguist Émile Benveniste makes an important distinction between what he calls the *polarity of person* and *non-person:* "There are utterances in discourse that escape the condition of person in spite of their individual nature, that is, they refer not to themselves but to an 'objective situation.' This is the domain we call the 'third person.'" The difference between polarity of person and nonperson is clear—in dialogue person is always reversible. I can become you, and you, I, while this is not true of he, she, and it. By moving the first person outside of dialogue, Wegg's *person* has become *nonperson*, a leap that brings me back to Mr. Inspector's earlier confusion about how he should address a dead man. The "I" bone, after all, is a corpse piece of Wegg, one that has made its way to the morgue a little earlier than the rest of him.

Wegg is only one of many characters in Dickens who has a body that has fallen apart. The novels abound with amputees, bloody messes, bodies that explode, disintegrate, or liquefy, as well as countless metaphorical references to going to pieces. In *Dombey and Son*, a train steams over Carker with "its fiery heat and cast his mutilated fragments into the air." In *Bleak House*, Krook spontaneously combusts. In *Oliver Twist*, Sikes leaves the murdered Nancy "a dark heap in a blood-stained room." In *Little Dorrit*, Blandois is crushed and found "in a dirty heap of rubbish," his head "shivered to atoms." In *Martin Chuzzlewit*, Joseph Willet loses an arm and Simon Tapertit's legs are crushed and replaced by wooden ones. In the unfinished *The Mystery of Edwin Drood*, it's obvious that Jasper has disposed of his nephew with quicklime, an acid that eats skin and bone. And this is the short list. The crushed body is a leitmotif in Dickens—an image central to the writer's imagination. In *Our Mutual Friend*, this destroyed corpse becomes the vehicle for the obsessive question: How does one construct a self?

Wegg's dearly departed leg is in the possession of Mr. Venus, a man in the business of articulating bones. I like to think that in this dingy bone shop Dickens gathered together all the smashed corpses from his earlier books and gave Venus the impossible task of rebuilding them. Venus faces three problems—seeing, recognizing, and finally identifying the fragments he has in front of him. Throughout the narrative, Dickens isolates each step, which echoes the realities of perception. In a dense fog I may *see* shapes in front of me but not *recognize* any of them, or, as often happens, I may recognize a face but can't *identify* it with a name. Venus, underworld Encyclopedist that he is, sets about trying to order the bits and pieces of the dead from what the narrator tells us is "a muddle of objects vaguely resembling pieces of leather and dry stick . . . among which nothing is resolvable into anything distinct." This "muddle" isn't limited to the bone shop; it is continually present in the story from its beginning. The novel opens in the gloom of twilight on the Thames. The narrator points out two people in an unmarked boat, which has "no identifying marks whatsoever." Four paragraphs later, the setting sun illuminates the craft's hull for an instant, and the reader catches a glimpse of "a rotten stain" that bears "some resemblance to the outline of a muffled human form." *Muffled* and *muddled* are words that pertain to the whole world of the book. Perceiving what's out there is difficult. Dust blows in the streets. Obscure figures appear and disappear. "Misty, misty, misty," says another character, Jenny Wren, as she tries to make sense of who is who and what is what in her own life. "Can't make it out."

Making out the world is a perceptual conundrum in *Our Mutual Friend*, and Mr. Venus's job is rebuilding splintered bodies. In a startling little parable about isolating, recognizing, and naming things, Mr. Venus gives Wegg a tour of his shop. "I've gone on improving myself," he says, "until by sight and by name I'm perfect."

> "A wice. Tools. Bones, warious. Skulls warious. Preserved Indian baby. African ditto . . . human warious. Cats. Articulated English baby. Dogs. Ducks. Glass eyes, warious. Mummied bird. Oh dear me, that's the general panoramic view." Having so held and waved the candle as all these heterogeneous objects seemed to come forward obediently when they were named and retire again.

The candle makes the objects visible and recognizable, but it is the names that seem to call forth each thing from the murk and make it legible. Venus articulates his anatomies in space and in language, creating sense from nonsense through categorization. Wegg expresses admiration for the anatomist's work by saying, "You with the patience to fit together on the wires the whole framework of society—I allude to the human skelinton." By collapsing the "framework of society" and the bones of the human body into one, Wegg again makes a brilliant hash of things. Of course people in society need their bones, but the wooden gentleman's allusion to this *framework* reverberates throughout the novel on two levels—how the body is represented visually in space and in language.

We all need to assemble ourselves, to have a working image or framework that we carry around with us as an inner representation of our own bodies, to which we attach an identity. Pathologies of body image, whether caused by lesions in the brain or emotional distress, make it clear that these representations are both essential and mysterious. "Phantom limb syndrome," for example, in which amputees feel the presence of a missing leg or arm, and often suffer pain in it, is a form of

Weggism. These people have an ongoing relationship with a part of them that has, in fact, disappeared. *Anosognosia*, another disorder, caused by damage to the right hemisphere of the brain, leaves patients unaware of what they've lost. They refuse to acknowledge what's obvious to others—that they're paralyzed or can't move their left hand, or whatever their handicap happens to be. Others are afflicted with a condition simply called "neglect." They ignore the left side of their bodies and the entire left side of space, as if it weren't there. People with severe neglect may even deny, against all reason, that an impaired arm or leg belongs to them—reverse Weggism. Anorexics, bulimics, as well as many people who wouldn't be considered clinically ill are also prone to deranged images of their own bodies. Contemporary Western culture is full of people who feel fat when they are actually thin, who obsess about their thighs and stomachs, their bags and their wrinkles, and even those who have a relatively stable body image are subject to mutations in their dreams. I lose parts of myself regularly when I'm asleep, often my teeth and hair, but I've also lost hands and feet. Distorted, partial, and broken visions of the body make it clear that these representations are far more precarious than we might like to think. It is precisely this inner fragility that Dickens maps with astounding acumen.

Wegg's allusion to *articulation* is double. Words are articulated as well as bones, and language might well be called "the framework of society," because it makes our collective life possible. In the world of the book, the word *society* refers to a specific group of characters, the most important of whom are the Podsnaps, the Lammles, and the Veneerings. Despite the fact that Mr. Venus's shop and fashionable society couldn't be more removed from each other in terms of the story, Dickens binds them metaphorically. They are linked by the morbid fragment, the piece or part, which, like Wegg's bone, refuses to be incorporated into a meaningful framework—the thing that cannot be articulated. "I can't work you into a miscellaneous one, nohow," Venus tells Wegg. "Do what I will, you can't be got to fit. Anybody with a passable knowledge would pick you out at a look, and say—No go! Don't match!"

In a scene at the Veneerings', Dickens's "society" is depicted as a broken anatomy, not seen directly but in a mirror. The long passage is written entirely in sentence fragments, as if the piecemeal nature of what the narrator is describing has invaded his syntax.

> Reflects mature young lady; raven locks and complexion that lights up well when well powdered—as it is carrying on considerably in the captivation of mature young gentleman; with too much nose in his face, too much ginger in his whiskers, too much torso in his waistcoat, too much sparkle in his studs, his eyes, his buttons, his talk and his teeth.

As a reader, I see a depthless field of reflected shards, in which torso and teeth are equivalent to studs, buttons, and even talk, an image that again evokes the bits and pieces of Mr. Venus's bone shop and his articulations of the "warious." By using a mirror, Dickens clearly wants to depict society as a world of surface, artifice, illusion, as a *veneer*, but he doesn't have to shatter the conventional boundaries of the body to do that. In fact, mirrors are the only place where we experience ourselves as a visual whole from the outside. The "I" takes the position of a "you." Most of the time we see ourselves only in parts, our hands moving in front of us, our arms, fingers, torso, or our knees and feet. This total view of the body in the mirror is what led the French psychoanalyst Jacques Lacan to posit his theoretical mirror stage, which for him meant the moment a child recognizes itself as a whole person in a reflection through the eyes of what he calls the Other, which is both a real other person and the whole symbolic landscape in which the child lives—namely language. Lacan was not Piaget. He wasn't a great observer of children, and I don't believe that his mirror stage corresponds to an actual event in the story of human development. Rather, it was his way of speaking to the fact that we as human beings are born without an awareness of our corporeal boundaries. Infants are fragmented beings who come together as whole selves only over time, and the borders and categories established in language are crucial to the creation of a separate and complete idea of the self. This psychoanalytic model of development that moves from a fragmentary to a whole body image becomes more potent as an idea when it is linked to cases of brain damage or mental illness like the ones I mentioned earlier. For Lacan, the person seen in the mirror represents a form of therapeutic wholeness, a kind of ideal body, one that is never completely achieved because it has been built over a substrata of fragmentation.

Whenever things are going to pieces in Dickens, the reader can be sure that identities are wobbling and the smell of death is in the air. A moribund quality pervades Dickensian *society*. These are people who, like Wegg's bone, escape articulation. The aged Lady Tippins, for example: "Whereabout in the bonnet and drapery announced by her name any fragment of the real woman may be concealed is perhaps known to her maid." When this bonnet-and-drapery shakes a fan, the noise is compared to the "rattling of bones," a sound that echoes a comment Eugene Wrayburn made earlier in the novel. Looking down at the bloated corpse of Radfoot, he quips, "Not much worse than Lady Tippins." The morsel on the traveler's plate is reincarnated in biting satire. The question is: How can you identify with a name what you can't make out?

Floating Signs

There is no magical connection between words and things, or as the Old Soldier put it in *David Copperfield*, "Without Dr. Johnson or somebody of that sort we might have been at this present moment calling an Italian iron a bedstead." Every once in a while, I find myself staring long and hard at a word I've written, a word like *than*, and I wonder what in heaven's name it means and if I have spelled it correctly. At moments like this I come face-to-face with the utterly arbitrary and mysterious character of language. The sign or, as semioticians would have it, the signifier, the inscribed letters *t-h-a-n*, seems to float away from meaning and sits there on the page in front of me, stark naked and absurd.

Our Mutual Friend is a book that insists on the chasm between words and things. The comedy of "Lady Tippins" is that this name, supposedly meant to designate a whole and visible person, refers instead to an ad hoc collection of mobile feminine accoutrements. Society, however, is indifferent to the world out there because it fetishizes the name over the referent. The fact that Tippins can't be made out at all is of little importance. When Veneering runs for Parliament, he hopes that the powerful Lord Snigsworth will "give his name as a member of my committee. I don't go so far as to ask for his Lordship; I ask only for his name." Veneering bribes his way into office, so that, the reader is told, "he may write a couple of initials after his name at the extremely cheap rate of two thousand five hun-

dred per letter." He exchanges pound notes for the letters *M.P.*
As the dominant cultural fiction of developed societies, money
is the ideal nonsensical sign. I have always found it amazing
that in exchange for paper I can get a book or a dress, that the
stock market actually rises and falls on rumor—mere talk—and
that people trade in something called Futures, as if such a thing
were possible. I accept that all this is part of my world, and yet
I continue to find it bizarre. Dickens obviously shared this baf-
flement. As powerful as it is, money refers to nothing real. Cur-
rency floats. Dickens reiterates Marx's idea of money as
society's founding gibberish, as "the general confounding and
compounding of all things—the world upside down." When
money is hoarded, it becomes even more meaningless because
it buys nothing. It just accumulates like so much wastepaper.

> Why money should be so precious to an ass so dull as to ex-
> change it for no other satisfaction, is strange; but there is no
> animal so sure to get laden with it, as the Ass who sees noth-
> ing written on the face of the earth as the three dry letters
> L.S.D. not Luxury, Sensuality, Dissoluteness, which they so
> often stand for, but the three dry letters.

In an age when designer *labels* and celebrity *names* are
used to sell everything from cars to lipstick, when meaningless slogans and lyrics and acronyms are constantly beamed
and displayed and written on screens and billboards and the
covers of magazines, when right-wing politicians hammer
out the same empty phrases ad nauseam, corrupting words
like *freedom* and *truth* until they are no longer recognizable
and refer to absolutely nothing, Dickens's satire on dry letters is hardly irrelevant to us. The ugly side of this is that

such nonsense has power when it is delivered in the guise of authority.

As a young man Dickens studied shorthand. He called the cryptic squiggles of this new alphabet "the most despotic characters I have ever known."

> The changes that were wrung upon dots which in such a position meant such a thing and in such another position meant something entirely different; the wonderful vagaries that were played by circles; the unaccountable consequences that resulted from marks like flies' legs, the tremendous effect of a curve in the wrong place, not only troubled my waking hours but reappeared before me in my sleep.

I have a similar relation to numbers. Algebra, in particular, remains impenetrable to me. Many people can remember struggling in school under the weight of some unfamiliar set of hieroglyphs they were supposed to master and being threatened with failure if they didn't. Children are expected to digest all sorts of arbitrary systems, and the demands from on high can be crushing. Despite the fact that he fathered ten children, Dickens, the writer, never gave up his position as a child. He identified with children and with the child-like—those who are not in power and who suffer under the fickle and often sadistic demands of those who are. The list of brutalized children in Dickens is so long that I could fill up pages with their names. But unlike *Nicholas Nickleby* or *David Copperfield*, where the miseries of having learning beaten into you by a cruel schoolmaster or stepfather are played out fully and poignantly in the stories of particular characters, *Our Mutual Friend* addresses the abstract nature of paternal authority itself.

The dead father, the missing father, the estranged father, and just the distant father are all figures of loss that reverberate deeply in life and in literature. Fathers are essentially different from mothers because we were all once in our mother's bodies, are born out of those bodies, and as infants take food from them. Paternity is more distant and less direct than maternity; it's a *claim* we accept as children, one inscribed in our legitimate, that is, legal, names. In *Our Mutual Friend,* a number of fathers never appear in the flesh— their bodies are out of the story. Like the letters and names that float in "society," the *paternal figures* in the book are also *figures of the paternal*—more despotic characters that children find indecipherable, difficult to understand or speak to. They appear as signs or images of the law that can't be addressed directly, because the person they refer to is either deaf to others or missing altogether. As a description of the law, this makes good sense. In societies that aren't absolute monarchies or dictatorships, the law doesn't reside in the body of a living person. It is *written*—inscribed in documents that proclaim rules, which carry the threat of punishment when broken.

Dickens's patriarchy—Lords, MPs, judges, and fathers— are by and large an inscrutable group. Some of them exist only as paper or letters. Harmon Senior, dead before the book begins, speaks through the multiple "last testaments" and codicils he hid around his property, each one dispensing his money in a different way. There is no final will, no coherent word, just contradictory edicts. Eugene Wrayburn's father appears only as an acronym, *M.R.F.* (Most Respected Father). In the imaginary arguments Eugene conducts with M.R.F., the internalized father crushes the son with his blanket prohibitions. Another character, Twemlow, has a father figure

as well, the tyrannical Lord Snigsworth, from whom Veneering solicits a *name* only. Like M.R.F., Snigsworth never appears bodily in the narrative. He is only represented by a
portrait that hangs on the wall. What we do know is that
when Twemlow visits Snigsworthy Park, he is put under "a
kind of martial law."

All written language has a ghostly aspect—the disembodied voice speaking to you from the page—but Dickens's paternal signs are also oppressive, fickle, and drained of meaning.
When the fathers speak, they use the language of a mad king
on a distant mountaintop issuing directives that merely con-
fuse the poor subjects below who are expected to act on them.
There is no dialogue with the fathers—the talk runs only one
way. It's easy to understand why Kafka admired Dickens so
much. K.'s peregrinations through alien corridors inhabited
by dirty bureaucrats and invisible authorities resonate strongly
with Dickens's bewildered children trying to locate and interpret the mysterious despotic signs hurled down at them from
above. These are the words of dead languages that disguise
rather then delineate reality. When Podsnap is told that six
people have starved to death in London, the bourgeois patri-
arch makes the familiar argument that they deserved it.
Twemlow, modest spokesman for the child's position, objects.
Podsnap swiftly accuses his guest of "Centralization." Twemlow manages to reply that "he was certainly more staggered
by these terrible events than he was by names, of howsoever
many syllables." *Centralization* is a word like *freedom*. In the
mouths of politicians, bureaucrats, and ideologues, it is used
to disguise the dead bodies that lie beneath it and the particular human stories that belong to each of those lost lives. At its
worst, this language is only noise. The twentieth century and
the new century we have now entered provide us with count-

less examples of ideological terms used to hide and distort the politics of neglect and murder.

Madness

When Dickens was writing *Our Mutual Friend*, he was also giving readings, performances his family and friends thought strained him to the breaking point and probably hastened his death. Over and over, Dickens performed what he and those close to him simply referred to as "the murder": Bill Sikes's murder of Nancy from *Oliver Twist*. "There was a fixed expression of horror of me all over the theater," Dickens wrote, "that couldn't have been surpassed if I had been going to be hanged." This was a period of disillusionment in Dickens's life, of sadness and a nagging emptiness. "What was there but the fearful stimulus of the readings," his biographer Edgar Johnson writes, "and returning to them as Jasper in *The Mystery of Edwin Drood* would return to the dangerous excitement of his drugged visions." The readings became a kind of opiate for Dickens, and as he performed he worked himself into a feverish trance of high emotion. Ladies fainted, men gasped, and when it was over the author would limp off the stage exhausted, tears streaming down his face. He played all the parts, Fagin, Sikes, and Nancy. As Nancy, he begged and screamed for his life; as Sikes, he mercilessly clubbed his victim to death. Writing novels means being plural, being divided among your creatures and suffering with them. While he was onstage, Dickens lost himself in his characters and the horror of what he was reading, and by all accounts it took a terrible toll on his health. In his biography, Peter Ackroyd notes that early in 1869 the author reported that he was "at present nightly murdered by Mr. W. Sikes" and around the same time also wrote in a letter to a friend, "I am murdering Nancy . . . I have a vague sensation of being 'wanted' when I walk the streets." Dickens's use of the first person is significant, if only because it demonstrates that these two beings were close enough to him to be "I."

Dickens continually explored extreme states of disintegration, and in *Our Mutual Friend* he created a character, Bradley Headstone, whose breakdown is in part presented as pathological repetition—the machine-like churning in his mind of an attempted murder. The connection to Dickens's own performances is striking. While Dickens's fictional character Headstone is guilty of a crime, and his creator was guilty only of invention and empathy for those inventions, Headstone nevertheless repeats the crime in his imagination long after it is over, just as Dickens couldn't resist performing his murder again and again. A powerfully imagined event can evoke the same emotions as a real event. Few artists would contradict this, and yet there are no doubt people who would find it odd that a fiction, when fully imagined, can create something parallel to the disruptions of mental illness. Dissolution in art is preferable to dissolution in madness, but what Freud called "sublimation" is the transformation of inner dramas, fears, and wounds into something else: a work of art outside the body of the artist. This is true for all arts except acting, in which the body is the instrument for transformation. There are parts of my books that I have never read aloud and never will—they are simply too painful for me. I resist embodying my own words and characters and prefer to keep them at a safe distance on the page. Dickens had long been reluctant to perform "the murder," but once he had witnessed the horrified response of his friends on whom he tried out his "reading," their shocked faces became the impetus for repetition. Bradley Headstone, the mad schoolmaster and criminal in *Our Mutual Friend*, is *not* a stand-in for Charles Dickens. I am suggesting something quite different: Dickens's reading obsession provides a window into the writer's personality and his plural and complex inner identifications—ones that included both *I am being murdered* and *I am murdering*.

In Bradley Headstone, the reader is presented with a character who suffers from what would now be called "psychosis." The language of psychiatry has changed over the years, and diagnosing a character in a novel is naïve at best, but Headstone's madness fascinates me because it broadly depicts clinical realities that have always been present in some forms of insanity. In his book *Aggression in Personality Disorders and Perversions*, Otto Kernberg states it simply: "There is a profound sense of loss or dispersal of identity in psychosis." Of course, *Our Mutual Friend* as a whole expresses both *a profound sense of loss* and *a dispersal of identity*, but it is not a psychotic text; it treats these losses coherently. Dr. Daniel Dorman, in his narrative account of a single schizophrenic patient, Catherine, relates that after she had sat in stony silence for nearly an entire session she announced just before it ended, "I am Humpty Dumpty, in pieces, and there is no way to put broken eggshells back together again. I am cracked up." Catherine's silence is as important as her final words. The shattered self must raise defenses or die, and words to express this state do not come easily. In Bradley Headstone, Dickens gives the reader a man whose plural inner turmoil brings him to violence and then tears him apart.

Headstone suffers from a radical disconnection between

his inner and outer self, his feelings and his words. Despite the monstrous struggles that are being waged inside him, his schoolteacher persona is dull, dry, and emotionless. This bifurcation between inner disturbance and external deadness also has a clinical dimension. One of my favorite stories about the English pediatrician and psychoanalyst D. W. Winnicott is told by M. Masud R. Khan in his introduction to Winnicott's book *Holding and Interpretation*. In 1971, near the end of his life, Winnicott met with a group of Anglican clergymen. The question they asked him was simple. They wanted to know how to distinguish between an ill person who needed psychiatric help and a person who could be helped by their counseling. Dr. Winnicott didn't answer immediately, but after some thought, he said: "If a person comes and talks to you and, listening to him, you feel he is boring you, then he is sick, and needs psychiatric treatment. But if he sustains your interest, no matter how grave his distress or conflict, then you can help him alright."

The brilliance of this comment is that it unearths a truth about many people who are mentally ill: In their preoccupation with what is happening inside them, they are walled off from other people, and this barrier prevents them from engaging another person in genuine conversation. The speaker's lack of connection inevitably creates boredom in the listener. Headstone, like Podsnap, like countless other characters in the novel, is shut off from language as *a means of communication with another person.* The symbols of paternal authority Dickens indicts with such fury reveal themselves through the telling adjective he uses to incriminate the letters: *dry.* Everybody knows what a dry text is—one that has left out feeling, one that bores you stiff because it doesn't speak to anything human, hides the obvious under obfuscation, or is simply incomprehensible.

> The exponent [Headstone] drawling on to My dear Childern-err, let us say for example about the beautiful coming to the Sepulchre; the repeating of the word Sepulchre (commonly used among infants) five hundred times and never once hinting what it meant.

In this evocation of Headstone's pedagogy, Dickens typically wrings every possible meaning out of the word *Sepulchre*. The reader knows the word means tomb, the receptacle for a dead body. The reader also knows that in the story being told, the tomb is empty when the women of the "beautiful coming" arrive. For the children who don't know the word's meaning, the letters themselves are vacant symbols, more verbiage coming from the mouth of their teacher. *Sepulchre* also points to the exponent issuing the nonsense, Headstone, a word that signifies a marker for the dead, a mere *name* aboveground announcing what once existed but has now become mere fragments of flesh and bone in the earth. Furthermore, the schoolmaster's lessons, like the word *Centralization*, disguise a "terrible event." The dull rhythms of his droning instruction become the frame for Headstone to relive his assault on Eugene, whom he has beaten to a bloody pulp and left for dead: "As he heard his classes he was always doing it again and improving on its manner, at prayers, in his mental arithmetic, all through his questioning, all through the day." Language is a veneer, beneath which lies pure inarticulate rage.

Headstone is caught in a treadmill of obsession, compelled to relive his crime again and again. The word *mechanical* is used several times to describe the schoolmaster, signaling a growing resemblance to machinery and the inanimate. Repetition is meaning. Without it there is no memory, no recognition, no language, but compulsive repetitions that won't allow for difference may also be a sign of sickness. In *Beyond the Pleasure Principle*, Freud first made the connection between the human urge to repeat and the death instinct. In the essay, he notes what every parent knows: Children never tire of playing the same games and hearing the same stories over and over and have little tolerance for even the slightest change. For Freud, this voracious appetite for identical repetition is the child's way of mastering his environment, but in adulthood the desire for this disappears. In his patients he noticed that their need to repeat childhood events "disregarded the pleasure principle in every way." The compulsion to return to the same thing time and again was actively self-destructive. In *Our Mutual Friend*, repetition without variation is both pathological and moribund. A character like Podsnap, whose entire existence is summarized in the routine "getting up at eight, shaving close at quarter past, breakfasting at nine, going to the City at ten, coming home at half past five, and dining at seven," is the bourgeois version of Headstone's insular cycle of *doing it again*. The rhythm that allows no change, no difference, is one that seeks to stop time, and stopping time means death. The teacher has lost the possibility of an ongoing story because he is trapped in the trauma of a single moment and is never released.

Headstone is the perpetrator of a crime against another person, not the victim, but his inner savagery partakes of both sides, not unlike Dickens's incarnation as both Sikes and Nancy. "The man was murderous and he knew it. More, he irritated it with a kind of perverse pleasure akin to which a man has in irritating a wound upon his body." Torturer and tortured occupy the same psychic ground. In the end, the school-master's body can't bear the strain, and it erupts. He loses control of his movements and suffers from spasms, nose-bleeds, and then seizures, epileptic fits he can't remember and which leave him completely drained. He loses control of his body in space, and his amnesia disrupts all sense of time. True to Dickens's storytelling, the ravages of this explosive inner campaign aren't confined within Headstone. They move out-ward onto the larger canvas of the novel and are acted out through others in disguise, doubling, and mistaken identity. This is the *written-ness* of Dickens, the dreaming, overdeter-mined quality of his work. Once unleashed, a Dickensian theme is unstoppable; it spreads and bleeds from one charac-ter and one story within the story into another.

In order to commit the crime, Headstone disguises himself as Rogue Riderhood, the "Waterside Character," and in these clothes he appears to be not less but more himself: "And whereas in his schoolmaster clothes he usually looked as if he were in the clothes of some other man, he now looked in the clothes of some other man or men, as if they were his own." He "owns" these clothes because they suit what has been hidden, the suppressed *other*. The inside has come out. The word *Other* becomes a signal in the novel that boundaries are tumbling and people are going to pieces. Riderhood dubs the schoolmaster "T'Otherest." He arrives at the name through three men he as-sociates in his mind: Lightwood, "The Governor"; Wrayburn, "T'Other Governor"; and Headstone, "T'Otherest Governor," who then becomes simply "T'Otherest." T'Otherest is an apt name for a double, but it also describes the extremity of Head-stone's position and alludes to his slide toward verbal incoher-ence and eventually *T'Other World,* a phrase Riderhood also uses—the place of death and decay. The two men serve as mirror selves, and this reflective quality is also a form of confusion, not only of identity—which one is which—but of an erosion of the line between inside and outside. When Riderhood sees the disguised Headstone float by him on a barge, he makes a remark that reverberates with the pronominal play in the book as a whole: "Never thought myself so good-looking afore." I am you. You are I.

Years ago, a psychiatrist told me a story I have never forgotten. Before a meeting with a schizophrenic patient, the doctor had been to the hairdresser and had her long hair cut short. When the patient entered the room for his session, he looked at her and said in a shocked voice, "You cut my hair!" "I" and "you" mingle in a single utterance that confuses self and other and echoes Riderhood's ironic comment that uses the word *myself* to designate his double. Such confusion isn't uncommon in schizophrenia, and this overlap is a familiar theme in works of literature where doubles and mirror images and ghostly selves appear and reappear. In his famous essay on the double, Otto Rank connected its insistent presence in art to the mirror image and death, and Dickens doesn't betray this theory. The reflected double is a harbinger of disintegration, both of the body and of words. When Bradley Headstone cries out, "I have been set aside and I have been cast out," the schoolmaster has reached the end of reciprocal speech—no dialogue is possible for him anymore. When he is near his end, the narrator tells us that Headstone has "trouble articulating his words." He stammers and hesitates and can't get them out. His language is falling apart, and these speech fragments, like the sentence fragments used to describe the mirror at the Veneerings', signal a self in bits and pieces. Like Humpty Dumpty, it is all cracked up. The reflected selves, Riderhood and Headstone, cannot remain separate. They fight to the death and end up in the river, where they drown, one corpse's limbs entangled in the other's.

Our Mutual Friend turns on this relation between the self and the other. The mirroring between the two can be sick and confused or more autonomous and healthy, but the novel never lets go of this dialectic. If the relation is cut, the self vanishes. Those who are walled off, isolated, and unrecognized drown. For me, this is a simple human truth, one that Dickens elaborates more fully and with greater subtlety than any writer I know. Although I have never been interested in narrow "readings" of books through the lens of this or that philosophy or system, the geography of the self and the other that Dickens maps in *Our Mutual Friend*, one that treats mirroring and the role of language, reverberates strongly with ideas in both psychoanalysis and neurobiology that seek answers to fundamental questions about human identity.

Winnicott, who read Lacan's essay on the mirror stage when it was published in 1949, grounded Lacan's idea of mirroring in his clinical experience of the relation between mother and child and bore witness to the fact that the child comes to recognize itself in the answering face of its mother. This dialectic bears a close relationship to Allan Shore's comment in his book *Affect Regulation and the Origin of the Self: The Neurobiology of Emotional Development:* "The early social environment, mediated by the primary caregiver, directly influences the evolution of structures in the brain responsible for the future socioemotional development of the child." In other words, the old dualism between nature and nurture is rendered moot. The outside also becomes us. A human being is born an unfinished organism and as the person develops experience with others becomes a physical reality. The *I* and the *you* are not as neatly separated as the culture likes to believe.

Language plays an essential part in our development, and brain research has begun to verify physically what linguists like Benveniste had codified long before. G. Rizzolatti's studies on monkeys led him to discover a class of neurons he calls "mirror neurons," which are activated in the brains of monkeys not only when they are performing certain actions like grasping or tearing but when they are watching the same activity in another monkey. Although Rizzolatti doesn't mention it, this seems closely related to the phenomenon in children called *transitivism*. Simply put: If one toddler falls down and starts crying, the child watching the tumble also begins to howl. In his article "Language Within Our Grasp," published in 1998, Rizzolatti and his fellow researchers argue that a similar neuronal action takes place in human beings in the left hemisphere of the brain and that this reflecting activity forms the foundation for language: "The development of the capacity of the observer to control his or her mirror system is crucial in order to emit (voluntarily) a signal. When this occurs a primitive dialogue is established. This dialogue forms the core of language." Mirroring makes speech possible; language relies on the reflective quality of *I* and *you* through which verbal interaction becomes possible.

In *Descartes' Error*, Antonio Damasio suggests that what we call the self is a representation of our organism that is continually regenerated in the brain: "The self is a repeatedly reconstructed biological state," and that what he designates as *subjectivity* is another *image* or *representation* of "an organism in the act of perceiving and responding to an object." Damasio does not say it explicitly, but this internal representation or brain image, which he delineates as subjectivity, is dialectical—*the image of a relation*. He doesn't confine it to the relation between "I" and "you" but includes all external objects as well. Damasio is less interested in the role of language in subjectivity than others and proposes a nonverbal narrative for the self. He does write, however, "Language may not be the source of the self, but it is certainly the source of the 'I.'" I don't think that the self is constituted in language but rather that language plays a vital role in perception and memory and necessarily mingles with an individual human narrative. Elizabeth Bates, who has been studying language and the brain at the University of California, San Diego, states it clearly: "The experience of language helps create the shape and structure of the mature brain."

"There Was No Such Thing as I"

Wegg's labile, necrotic *I* reflects an anxiety he is able to express perfectly: "I should not like—under any circumstances, to be what I may call dispersed, a part of me here and a part of me there, but I should wish to collect myself like a genteel person." Mr. Dolls, a minor character in the novel and a shuddering alcoholic wreck, cannot collect himself at all. His *I* doesn't wander like Wegg's. It has disappeared altogether. "Circumstances over which had no control," Dolls mutters repeatedly, and, resorting to the third person, "Poor shattered invalid. Trouble nobody long." Faithful to the book's logic, the narrator refers to Dolls as *it*, not *he*. And, like Headstone, Dolls has a mechanical aspect: "The very breathing of the figure was contemptible as it laboured and rattled in that operation like a blundering clock." Dolls's *I* has gone underground, buried there with his real name—Cleaver, another word among many that suggest cutting and shredding. Mr. Dolls is

a nickname given to him by Eugene Wrayburn because the
ruin's daughter is "the dolls' dressmaker," Jenny Wren. Mr.
Dolls's first-person pronoun has been drowned in drink, and
without it he can't engage another person directly. Dolls is a
grown-up who behaves like a child. His daughter Jenny never
calls him "you" or "father." She prefers the infantile and more
accurate "Bad Boy." Young children often refer to themselves
in the third person before they master the mysterious flux of
the *I,* and Dickens's novel is uncannily perceptive about this
pronoun. In its pages the *I* is never taken for granted.

How does a person lead a coherent life with a stable self,
whatever that self may be? *Our Mutual Friend* proposes a
route to a whole or more or less whole self through memory,
mirroring recognition, dialogue, and finally telling and fiction. As the connective tissue of time, memory is certainly essential to the internal narrative we create for ourselves. When
I was hospitalized for a migraine in 1983, I was in a bed in
the neurology ward at Mount Sinai Hospital across from a
woman who had suffered a severe stroke. She spoke rarely
and only in fragments. Every day her husband came to visit
her, but she had lost the ability to recognize him. She was a
tough old lady who escaped the fetters the nurses bound her
with every night, but she had no self that existed from one
moment to another—no story over time. That had vanished. A
number of years ago, a woman contacted my husband and
told him the story of her husband, a gifted composer and mu-
sician, whose memory was destroyed by meningitis. He kept a
notebook, and in it he wrote hundreds and hundreds of times
the same exclamation, "12:00. Where am I? 12:01. Where am
I? 12:02. Where am I?" And on and on. Trapped in the night-
mare of eternal repetition, he was unable to connect one
minute to another but retained enough self-consciousness in

those isolated moments to feel his disorientation. It is hard to think of a worse plight than living in a state of continual agony without any context for it. For this man, time had lost all meaning.

One of the most moving accounts of a man's struggles to regain a continuous identity is recorded in A. R. Luria's *The Man with a Shattered World*. Luria's patient, Zazetsky, was injured during World War II. Shell fragments damaged the left occipito-parietal region of his brain, leaving him with severe amnesia and aphasia. His field of vision was destroyed, and he had great difficulty recognizing objects, and even when he did recognize them, he often couldn't name them. He also lost both sight and awareness of the right side of his body, suffered from severe body-image distortions, and discovered to his horror that he could no longer read. Despite his grotesque handicaps, he relearned the alphabet and attained a level of literacy. Remarkably enough, he was still able to write—especially if he didn't lift his hand from the paper. Despite the fact that he had tremendous difficulty both remembering and reading what he had written, he recorded memories and experiences from his life. "It's depressing," he wrote, "having to start all over and make sense out of a world you've lost because of injury and illness, to get these bits and pieces to add up to a coherent whole." Zazetsky clung to the idea of a whole, and he worked doggedly to try to create meaning from his memories despite the excruciating slowness of his task, but both his doctor, Luria, and Zazetsky himself make it clear that the fragmented reality of his daily life didn't improve with time. He worked on the project until his death.

Unlike the stroke patient I met in the hospital, Zazetsky was painfully aware of what had happened to him—his self-consciousness remained intact. He had a recognizable self, but it was in tatters. Karen Kaplan-Solms and Mark Solms write about a patient with Wernicke's aphasia in their book *Clinical Studies in Neuro-Psychoanalysis*, a woman who, like Zazetsky, was keenly aware of her affliction. "Oh yes," Mrs. K. is quoted as saying, "I am in bits and pieces. I am in bits and pieces throughout my mind." These morbid "bits and pieces" and the attempt to rebuild them into a coherent structure *through language* reverberate strongly with the central drama of *Our Mutual Friend*.

Drowning or almost drowning in the Thames means entering a frightening broken space that has slipping borders and in which things and bodies can't be distinguished from one another, a place that is metaphorically connected to epilepsy in Headstone and to delirium in Eugene Wrayburn. After Eugene is saved by Lizzie from the Thames, the narrator tells us that his face has been so mutilated that his own mother wouldn't have recognized him. While he is unconscious, Eugene's feverish utterances are compared to "the frequent rising of a drowning man from the deep." But then, in a moment of clarity, he says, "When you see me wandering away from this refuge that I have so ill deserved, speak to me by my name, and I think I shall come back." This calling of a name echoes Mr. Venus's tour of his articulated bodies and again has a parallel in clinical experience. In *Awakenings*, Oliver Sacks describes what he calls "lucid intervals":

At such times—despite the presence of massive functional or structural disturbances to the brain—the patient is suddenly and completely restored to himself. One observes this, again and again, at the height of toxic, febrile or other deliria: sometimes a person may be recalled to himself by the calling

of his name; then for a moment or a few minutes, he is himself, before he is carried off into delirium again.

In *Our Mutual Friend,* the act of calling someone by name
is invested with this same restorative magic, one that prom-
ises at least temporary cohesion. Because a proper name is
the symbolic site of the self in language, it is the linguistic
marker of a collective, not private, reality. As such, it serves as
a way out of unconsciousness or, in terms of the book's literal
and metaphorical drowning, a way *up* to the surface and from
there *out* to other people. A word is essentially distinct from a
visual image inside us because, when we speak, we hear ourselves speaking. By crossing the border of the body, a word is
literally inside and outside us at the same time. The names our
parents gave us mark us for life, providing a sign of continuity
that yokes an unlikely pair—infant and old man. Names are
powerful, and Sacks is right: Their utterance can bring you
back or keep you awake.

Immediately after my car crash, I looked to see if I was
whole and miraculously discovered that I was. Nevertheless, I
froze. I didn't move. I think I could have, but I didn't. I knew
that my husband and daughter had managed to get out on the
other side of the car, and I must have been relieved that they
were okay, but I don't recall feeling this. Instead, I felt entirely
empty, very, very calm, and after some time—I have no idea
how long—my vision dimmed and grayed and I felt myself going under. Then, as if by magic, there was a man speaking to
me. He reached in through the broken window from the side,
put his hands on my face, and told me not to move my neck. I
remember he said he was a paramedic who just happened to
be walking by and that he had seen the accident. "I'm losing
consciousness," I said to him. "What is your name?" he said. I

told him. "What day is it?" I told him. He asked me my name again, and I told him again. I am convinced that this simple dialogue, combined with the stabilizing touch of his hands, kept me conscious until the firemen arrived.

Eugene is repeatedly called back by Lizzie, but in his semi-conscious mutterings he seems to be searching for another word he can't find. Jenny Wren gives it to Mortimer Light-wood, who then passes it on to Eugene. The word is *wife*. Eugene's movement is from unrecognizable near-corpse, a not-I, to being named and identified as a person who belongs to other people. Exactly the same threefold movement occurs in two short sentences spoken by Lucy Manette in *A Tale of Two Cities*. A door is opened onto the broken figure of a man, a man who has been confined to darkness in a tower cell for many years, a man who has forgotten his former life and his own name, a man with a voice so thin from disuse that it is "like a voice underground." When she first sees this ruined person, Lucy says, "I am afraid of it," and then a moment later, "I mean of him, my father." The Dickensian shift from *it* to *him* takes a third step to include *my father*. Like *wife*, *father* articulates a human connection, and through this spoken bond a process of reclamation and recollection begins. This is the *mutuality* announced by the book's title. The words *Our Mutual Friend* go beyond duality. They imply at the very least three people.

A crucial moment in the novel occurs when the hero, John Harmon, tries to piece together the story of his own near death, a story that took place before the novel begins, and after he has been living a painful pseudononymous existence for some time. "A spirit that once was a man could hardly feel stranger or lonelier going unrecognized among mankind than I feel." As the son of a punitive but indecisive father and a long dead mother, Harmon lives a ghostly borderline existence because he is unwilling to claim his rightful name by accepting his father's will. He can't be called back into a family. He returns to England "divided in my mind *afraid of myself*." The self he fears is incarnated in the double, Radfoot, a man with whom he has been confused on board the ship that takes him home. Headstone's inner division ends in death. Harmon nearly drowns, but he eventually manages to reunify his torn being. His monologue marks the beginning of that reconstruction:

> Now I pass to sick and deranged impressions; they are so strong that I rely upon them; but there are spaces between them I know nothing about, and they are not pervaded by any idea of time.
>
> I had drunk some coffee, when to my sense of sight he began to swell immensely . . . We had a struggle near the door . . . I dropped down. Lying helpless on the ground I was turned over by a foot . . . I saw the figure like myself lying on a bed. What might have been, for anything I knew, a silence of days, weeks, months, years, was broken by a violent wrestling of men all over the room. The figure like myself was assailed and my valise was in its hand. I was trodden upon and fallen over. I heard the noise of blows, and thought it was a woodcutter cutting down a tree. I could not have said that my name was John Harmon—I could not have thought it—I didn't know it—but when I heard the blows, I thought of a woodcutter and his axe, and had some dead idea that I was lying in a forest.
>
> This is still correct? Still correct, with the exception that I cannot possibly express it to myself without using the word I. But it was not I. There was no such thing as I, within my knowledge.

It was only after a downward slide through something like a tube, and then a great noise and a sparkling and crackling as of fires, that the consciousness came upon me, This is John Harmon drowning! John Harmon struggle for your life! John Harmon call on heaven and save yourself! I think I cried it aloud in a great agony, and then a heavy, horrid unintelligible something vanished, and it was I who was struggling there alone in the water!

Harmon's telling is an agonized *re-collection* of the events that led to his near drowning, during which he loses himself as subject of the story he wants so badly to remember: "There was no such thing as I." The monologue includes more wood and cutting imagery and a bizarre slide through "a tube" that precedes his regained consciousness. At first, Harmon is divided between the mirrored *figure like myself* (Radfoot) and the *I*. After the birth-like slide, his name returns to him, but he calls out to himself as if he were *somebody else* and addresses that other as *you*: "Struggle for *your* life!" Only after he has recognized himself as another, a separate and distinct whole being, does the corpse vanish, and he is able to assume the first person and his own story. In order for the self to exist, it must be able to represent itself as another, a mirror image, and the recognition of that whole self gives birth to the subject.

The fear of contamination Dickens's traveler has for the dead body that keeps returning to him in his imagination has escalated in Harmon's speech to the terror of complete annihilation. The abject weight that disappears underwater is no longer "I" or "you" but "it"—the not-I, or no longer I, not an *other* but an *otherest*. Harmon's speech is the account of a man trying to pull himself together by remembering, despite the fact that his memory is both marred by the distortions of hallucination and filled with the holes of unconsciousness. The telling takes the form of an internal dialogue during which the speaker interrogates himself, "This is still correct?" As with Zazetsky's need to record the fragments of his life on the page, Harmon arranges pieces of the past to articulate some kind of order despite his unstable state of mind. Drugged, beaten, intermittently unconscious, and then thrown overboard into the water, Harmon admits that his reflections are "deranged." He has carried these sick impressions or memories around with him for some time, and remembering them isn't enough; it's the telling or reconstruction of the pieces that is therapeutic and eventually reassembles an identity.

It's important to stress that the absence of a continuous self-narrative isn't only pathological—the result of psychotic breaks, brain damage, drugs, or near-death experiences. Normal life includes making sense of fragmentary memories. As Henry Adams writes in *The Education*, "His identity, if one could call a bundle of disconnected memories an identity, seems to remain; but his life was once more broken into separate pieces." We all collect and re-collect these pieces through self-image, memory, and language. I have long felt the cleft between my inner memories and the telling of them. My own recollections usually appear as images accompanied perhaps by a sentence or sentences spoken by another person or by me, moments that for one reason or another are entrenched in my mind, but fuzzy patches or large gaps remain. Yet another corpse story will serve as an illustration. I remember seeing Mao Tse-tung's preserved body in China in 1986. I have a picture of the waxy dead man in my mind, but it is no longer perfect, and I can't recall exactly how he, or rather *it*, was displayed. It was a peculiar experience but not a scary one. The

body looked too unreal for that. I have a visual impression of
the people around me—my sisters, friends, our Chinese
guide, and others waiting on line—but they are not precisely
drawn. I do remember clearly that my friend Eric said to me,
"Why are hundreds of people waiting for hours to see his
body?" Without thinking, I replied, "They want to make sure
he's *really* dead." Our guide, who had suffered a humiliating
and painful exile to the countryside during the Cultural Revolution, started to laugh, and in her hilarity she began to pound
me on the back. I remember the feeling of her hand hitting
my lower spine, but I could no longer give you a description
of her face. When I tell the story, however, I rely on the context of the experience and on the conventions of language, on
syntax, to turn the bits of memory into a narrative that has
the appearance of something far more whole than the various
pictures in my brain. After I had told the story several times,
the telling began to supplant the images. I had *learned* how to
tell it, and my narrative of that little incident has taken on a
solidity that my real memories don't have.

It is interesting that this new fixity arrives only through the
task of giving the story to another person. Memories that have
never been told aren't yet solid stories; they are potential stories. It may be that the interlocutor is the self, as in John Harmon's monologue, but it is always the self in relation to the
idea of another, the "I" addressing a "you," because the desire
to tell implies that the tale must become comprehensible to a
listener. Zazetsky wrote both for himself as an other and for
real others. He hoped that his descriptions of his illness
would be of use to those studying brain injury, and in this he
triumphed: His writing has proved invaluable to researchers.
It is this dialogical character of speech and storytelling that
Dickens insists on as *living*, not *dead*, language. Through his

telling, Harmon recovers the *I* Headstone loses. The only time Mr. Dolls says the word *I* in the novel is when he asks Eugene Wrayburn for a few pence to buy a drink. However pathetic Dolls's request, he is engaged in a real dialogue and receives an answer. For a brief moment, he has situated himself in the axis of discourse and emerges as a subject.

Harmon's full rehabilitation will come later in the novel. Mrs. Boffin, who acted as a surrogate mother to Harmon when he was young, is subject to strange visions of faces in the decrepit mansion where the boy grew up with his sister. One night Mrs. Boffin sees them everywhere: "For a moment it was the old man's, and then it got younger. For a moment it was both the children's, and then it got older. For a moment it was a strange face, and then it was all the faces." The strange face belongs to the ghostly hero of the novel, and when Mrs. Boffin fills in that blank, she brings the unrecognized spirit back from the dead and is able to call him by name. She also situates him in a narrative that is beyond himself, one that includes his father and images of generational resemblance that link parents and children in a mirroring vision over time.

The Magic of Fiction

The novel charts a course that moves back and forth between the unrecognizable, unnamed, unconscious drowned no-body to the recognizable somebody who is a conscious, speaking subject. We all travel a path that moves from the relatively oblivious and fragmentary state of infancy to a working internal image of the self, to a conscious, articulated "I" within the structures of language. Nobody has actual memories of in-

trauterine life or early infancy, but we experienced it nevertheless, and traces of that floating undifferentiated world remain in us and return to haunt us even in the everyday—in
fears, anxieties, longings, sex, sleep, and nameless sorrows. It
is part of a corporeal life that is mostly hidden from us, and
nothing is further from that early experience than the attempt
to inscribe that reality or some version of it in writing. And
yet I think this is what Dickens was drawn to—that fragmentary unformed space, or what I've often thought of as the *underneath*. In hallucinations, in psychoses, in various forms of
brain damage, in dreams, and in some moments of making
art, the underneath seems to roar to the surface: Whole pictures disintegrate and time is disrupted. This story we call the
self and articulate as *I*, Dickens tells us, is fraught and fragile,
and we must fight to keep it together.

The human experience of the world is not direct but mediated through what Wegg calls the "framework of society." This
framework is inescapable and necessary, but its articulations
may also be seen as the ordering fictions that make life livable. Both whole object representations in the brain, which
organize things in space, and language, which reorganizes
that material sequentially through abstract symbols, serve as
internal shields from the assault of stimuli coming from the
real world. They provide us with categories that create the
borders of perception and through expectation give external
reality both shape and sense, a truth that many artists,
philosophers, linguists, and psychologists have long intuited.
Without these shields we would be unable to construct an internal representation of a self. Brain scientists have located
these two dynamic structures, the spatial (right hemisphere)
and the audio-verbal (left hemisphere), but for me what is fas-
cinating is that Dickens seems to have glimpsed what the

world would be like without these protections, that fragmented, inchoate reality we all must have experienced as infants before our brains had structured that external "stuff" into things and words. It seems obvious that because our genetic identities and personal histories are all different, our brains, while similar to one another, are also unique. In other words, some people are more sensitive to stimuli than others. They feel what's happening inside and outside themselves. Dickens was one of these people. He understood or rather felt what Karen Kaplan-Solms and Mark Solms describe, using words that echo Dickens's own. "From a subjective viewpoint, an excited state of arousal in which the organism is forced to respond equally to all stimuli necessarily produces ego-fragmentation or annihilation. The 'I' is overwhelmed by a multitude of 'its.'"

We are always accommodating *its* into articulated frameworks that make life livable, but there are times when that integration fails, when the bone, as Mr. Venus says, won't fit, nohow. I think of these moments or states as holes in the structure—windows onto nonsense. We all long for fixity—and for some of us it's found in writing. Zazetsky's desire to record what he could of his life was sparked by a need to fill in the holes, to re-create coherence from what refused to cohere and to make his account sensible to a reader outside himself. Whatever its strengths or weaknesses, a written text has a solidity and permanence that spoken language can't have. We forget or misremember conversations, but a book can be quoted again with assurance. It doesn't change. In *Our Mutual Friend*, Dickens includes a tacit acknowledgment of his own fiction as a response to a shattered reality that is both outside and inside the self and a desire to make whole what has been broken in space and time. His artist is a crippled visionary child—Jenny Wren, once Fanny Cleaver, who has reinvented herself as an unhurt, airborne, fictional being. Like a novelist, she has characters—her dolls—whom she moves through stories borrowed from the known vocabulary of fairy tales and whom she dresses in scraps of fabric, which are referred to as "damage and waste." Jenny Wren's fictions are born from this damage, and although they don't allow her to throw her crutch away, in her reveries and stories she is whole and uninjured.

Dickens was preternaturally sensitive to distortions of language. He knew that words could be used as a tool for obfuscation, hypocrisy, and self-deception. He also knew that language was arbitrary and limited, that there were parts of human experience where words fall apart—in the choked stammerings of loss, of madness and delirium, and when we come close to the reality of our own inevitable deaths. He knew that the memory of every person is broken, interrupted by lapses and silences, and that our wholeness and continuity aren't givens but made in us and by us. He knew deeply that the self is an entity under threat and the trick of piecing it together isn't a solitary game. It is rooted in the other, where we find a mirroring wholeness, dialogue, and finally story. The journey in the book is from "it" to "I" to "We." This Dickensian *We* is language itself and the essential stories made from it, which not only bind us together but make sense of the world out there and keep the morbid fragment at bay.

2004

Extracts from a Story of the Wounded Self

THE FIRST STORY BELONGS TO MY MOTHER. SHE IS THE ONE who tells it, and when she tells it, she always includes a single terrible moment. She was at home taking a bath, and she thought to herself, How is it possible for a person to be as sad as I am? My mother was miserable because I was born too early. My lungs were undeveloped, and the doctor told my parents I might die. For two weeks, I lay in an incubator while my mother and father waited for my fate to be decided. In those days, the nurses didn't touch or massage babies left in incubators. I was separated from my mother in the first days of my life, and I now think that experience marks the beginning of a particular personality. When I suffered from convulsions on the day of my christening party, I scared my mother yet again. If I felt warm, my mother grew alarmed, and a single sound from my crib brought her to me. I was the firstborn child of a loving mother who lived in fear that she might lose me. We can't remember our infancies, but they live in our bodies, and had I not been frail at birth, I would have been someone else, and I would have had other thoughts. When I look back, I can't remember a time when I didn't carry around inside me a sensation of being wounded. The feeling ranges from the very slight to the acute, but the ache in my chest, dim or strong, has remained a constant in my life.

It is night, and I am lying in bed. Above me I notice a large drill thrust into the wall. No one is holding it; it begins to turn on its own, and as it turns, I see that long, thin cracks are forming in the wall. The cracks get larger, and then the wall begins to break open. I am overwhelmed with terror and throw myself against the wall to try to keep the fragments together, to stop the wall from collapsing. I'm screaming. I wake my mother. She remembers the night vividly and says that I must have woken my younger sister Liv, who panicked and also began to shriek. When my mother entered the room, we were both howling in fear. She said I had thrown myself against the wall and it looked as if I were trying to climb it. I don't remember Liv or my mother, but I remember the gaping fissures in the plaster and the revolving drill as if it had happened yesterday. I thought I was awake, but it must have been a dream, one without a threshold—I occupied the same place in the dream and in reality. The fear has never diminished in memory. I must have been about five years old.

This dream, hallucination, or night terror has haunted me as an adult because it is so simple, nearly abstract in its purity, and like no other in my experience. The bulk of my dreams as a child were long, shifting narratives with witches and ogres and people I knew that took place in streets and meadows and rooms and corridors. The crumbling wall remains an efficient metaphorical expression for both my obscure but omnipresent wound and the fear that often accompanies it. I'm afraid that thresholds and boundaries won't hold, that things will go to pieces.

My sister Liv and I left our mother and father for the first time to visit our grandfather's cousin in his little house in Highwood, just outside Chicago. After what was probably a week of our pining for her, our mother came to see us and then a couple of days later take us home by train. If I'm not mistaken, it was a cloudy afternoon. I remember how glad I felt as the three of us walked together through downtown Chicago and the feeling of my hand in my mother's. On our way, we crossed a bridge and saw two policemen restraining a man who had apparently climbed over the railing. Whether my mother said that the man had been intending to jump off the bridge or I simply knew it I can't say, but the officers and the desperate man made me feel the city's danger, and I found that air of menace more inspiring than upsetting. Very soon after that, we turned onto a sidewalk. There was a large gray building to my left, and to my right a crowd of people had gathered around someone lying on the pavement. I know it was a woman, but I have no memory of her. I can't see her face or body anymore. My mother, Liv, and I all looked at her, because I remember my mother's distress at the thought that we had seen her. When we walked away, my mother explained that the woman was having "an epileptic seizure" and couldn't help what was happening to her. We then crossed a wide street on our way to have lunch at Marshall Field's department store. The light was green and we began to walk, but in the middle of our crossing it changed to red and the cars moved forward as if we weren't there. This amazed me. My visual memory of that intersection, the cars, the looming building across from us, and the arching ramp above is exceedingly vivid. It may be that what I had witnessed immediately before, a chaotic body, heightened my recollection of what came afterward—the chaotic street. The honking cars that suddenly whizzed past us replaced the other, more threatening image of a woman who had lost control of herself.

In my first novel, I included an epileptic seizure witnessed from the roof of a building in New York. In the book, the woman's convulsive movements are photographed by one of the characters, and I now wonder if I wasn't returning to that street in Chicago and recording in fiction what I was unable to remember in fact. I am not an epileptic, but the shuddering body I saw must have echoed some tremor in myself, and it frightened me enough to swallow the picture whole and leave in its place an absence filled only by my mother's words *epileptic seizure*.

Like many children, I was prone to inward reveries—long dreaming sessions in which I would lose myself and look out at the world. How strange it is, I would think, that we see and smell and speak and eat and feel, that there are trees and cars and houses, barbed wire, cornfields, and cows. These thoughts were accompanied by a lifting within me that I experienced vaguely as closeness to God and nature (the two mingled in my mind) and as a form of private magic, a secret belief in my own power that set me apart from other people and would take me very far in the world. I have often wondered where this inner conviction came from. I was in no way a prodigious child. My early memories of school are mostly sad ones. I learned to read easily but suffered terribly over numbers. Even now, I cringe when I remember the long rows of intractable digits that never came out right. The complex relations among children—the ins and outs of friendships and alliances, the hierarchies of dominance and weakness on the school ground—puzzled and often hurt me. I wasn't athletic either, a serious deficit in most places but probably even more so in the Midwest, where physical prowess could catapult both boys and girls into a heroic position among their peers.

And yet, despite evidence to the contrary, I held fiercely to the lonely idea of my own great destiny, and I suspect that I clung to this irrational position for a single reason: my parents loved me very well. It was plain that my mother and my father thought I was wonderful. They made me feel that nothing was beyond me, and their belief in me and in my three younger sisters was unshakeable, a fortress into which we could retreat whenever we needed it. Years would pass before I understood that I came from a family that was remarkable in this respect, not ordinary. We are, all of us, made from our parents, physically and emotionally, and the quality we call "character" partakes of both genetic givens and the mysterious meanderings of a particular psychic history.

Some people are more prone than others to numinous experience—those moments or minutes of transcendence, disassociation, or euphoria. It seems clear to me now that I had a neurological as well as an emotional predisposition to these curious transports of the spirit. As a child I suffered from headaches, and at eight I remember my shock when a friend told me she had never had one. All my life, I have shivered at the mere sight of an ice cube, even on a sweltering day. Little more than a passing thought about ice produces a genuine shudder of cold in me. I once asked a neurologist about this, but he seemed not to know what I was talking about. Around the age of eleven, I suffered from commanding inner voices and rhythms that terrified me with their insistence. They always came when I was alone, and they seemed to want to impose their will on me, to press my body into their marching orders. The danger of madness seemed very real to me then, and I'm lucky they vanished. When I was twenty, I was struck with my first migraine, which lasted for eight months and then lifted. In the years that followed, it became obvious that my nervous system was unstable. I lived with auras that ranged from the very mild—a few black spots and brilliant white lights—to the more dramatic, such as a sudden seizure in my arm that hurled me against a wall. Once, I was subject to the very curious phenomenon known as "Lilliputian hallucinations," during which I saw a small pink man and his little pink ox on the floor of my bedroom and believed they were actually there. I have also had several euphoric episodes before getting sick, and despite the inevitable aftermath, I recall these moments with pleasure: My vision takes on a sudden heightened clarity that makes me imagine I am seeing what I normally can't, and then, just as I remark to myself on the fantastic quality of my eyesight, I feel an overwhelming joy.

Common wisdom designates this kind of happiness as aberrant, false, a mere trick of the brain that heralds an oncoming migraine or seizure, and there is some truth in this, but the experience is as real as any other, and it may be that trying to disentangle any emotion from the nervous system is futile. It is the interpretation that matters. However morbid my sensitivities may be, they are inseparable from the story of myself, and my reading of these peculiarities over time has been decisive in determining who I was and am.

I don't remember having any "rules" at home. We had routines that my three sisters and I accepted without question: getting up and eating breakfast, brushing our teeth, dressing for school, doing our homework, and going to bed early. Although we were sometimes scolded, we weren't punished. A look of disappointment in my mother's or father's eyes was usually enough to prompt a heartfelt apology from a momentarily wayward daughter. School, on the other hand, was all regulations, prohibitions, and punishments. I was well behaved, not only because I dreaded the cloakroom where children were rumored to be beaten but because I believed in an idea of goodness. I wanted to be pure, truthful—a diminutive saint. It's a good thing I wasn't an only child. My three younger sisters did me a great service when they laughed at my pious notions, my seriousness, my overdeveloped need to be responsible, conscientious, perfect. I'm afraid this unattractive portrait of my earlier self is accurate. I felt so much all the time that I longed for a way to order my inner tumult. Although I was a kind child, I could also be a rigid, humorless little person who took almost everything too hard. I wish I could say these flaws in my character have vanished, but that would be a lie. I remain attached to order, to moral thresholds, to all the forms that keep chaos at bay.

At Longfellow Elementary School, talking in the lunchroom was forbidden. Not even a whisper was tolerated. We ate in silence. If the rule was broken, the miscreant was sent to the far end of the room by an adult person known as a "lunchroom monitor" to eat at one of the brown tables with folding chairs. The tables for good children were white with long, smooth benches. The world of the brown tables was a remote place, inhabited by the naughty, the restless, the high-spirited—mostly boys who hadn't mastered the art of keeping quiet. I was in the first half of my second-grade year when it happened to me. The school principal, an intimidating, immensely tall person with the uncannily apt name of Mr. Lord, strode into the lunchroom to deliver an announcement. He began speaking, stopped suddenly in mid-sentence, and, to my horror, pointed in my direction. "You!" he bellowed. "Go to the brown tables!" I was stunned. I hadn't uttered a word. I had done nothing, but I picked up my tray and made the long, mortifying journey past the other children to take the brown seat of humiliation.

I was so troubled by the incident that I mustered the courage to speak to Mr. Lord on the playground after lunch. I walked toward him, looked up at his face, and said, "What did I do? I wasn't talking." I detected embarrassment and discomfort in his expression. He hesitated, and in that brief moment when he said nothing, I could already feel my triumph. He peered down at me without looking me in the eyes and muttered, *"You were swallowing your food while I was talking."* I was seven years old, and I knew this was ridiculous. He was ridiculous. The sentence burned itself into my consciousness as a sign of absolute sadistic stupidity. It had the force of an inner revelation: Some adults are as mean as some children. It was my innocence that had given me the strength to speak up and my innocence coupled with the Stalinist whims of Mr. Lord that removed every trace of humiliation from my trip to the brown tables.

My internal moral compass was extremely sensitive, however, and that same year I did something that tormented me for a long time afterward because the sin I may or may not have committed hinged on the interpretation of a single word. The class was doing arithmetic problems. As usual, I was struggling with the little numbers and the dreaded subtraction sign, which for some reason was so much worse than its friendlier companion, the plus sign. Our teacher, Mrs. G., left the room, and after she was gone, I realized I had to pee. I paused for a moment, then stood up and walked downstairs to the lavatory. My memory of that walk includes no feeling that I was doing anything particularly wrong. It's almost dream-like now. I wandered into the murky green hallway, made my way down the steps, peed alone in the little toilet stall, and then walked out the door marked GIRLS. As I left, I saw Mrs. G. straight ahead of me. It was time for the official bathroom break, and she was leading the class down the steps in two lines. She looked me in the eye and said, *"Was it an emergency?"* I said, "Yes." Immediately after I had spoken and for years to come, I asked myself whether I had lied. It wasn't really an emergency in the true sense of the word, was it? Could I have held my pee? Probably. Would it have been hard? Maybe. Did just having to go pretty badly constitute an emergency?

As an adult, I can tell myself that treating schoolchildren like prison inmates is bad pedagogy, that the half-lie may have saved me from a scolding or worse, but the story's interest lies in my struggle over semantics and the moral resonance of interpreting the meaning of a word. Had Mrs. G. not used the word *emergency*, I never would have remembered the incident. Some words, sentences, and phrases sit forever in the mind like brain tattoos. On the playground, children used to sing the chorus "Sticks and stones may break my bones, but words can never hurt me." Few things then or now have ever struck me as more false than that ludicrous chant. Words can devastate, and they can heal.

I don't have a picture in my mind of our Sunday school teacher reading the story of Abraham and Isaac to the class. I can't remember what she looked like and I don't recall her name, so I'll call her Mrs. Y. I retain a vague memory of light coming through a window and floating specks of dust in the air, but that might be from another class and another year at St. John's Lutheran Church. I do know we heard the story and that it alarmed me even before the teacher uttered these words: *"You have to love God more than anyone or anything."* "More than your parents?" I asked her. *"Yes."*

That "yes" tortured me for days. What kind of a God asked a man to kill his own son? What if God asked *me* to kill *my* parents? I could never do it. I knew I loved them far more than I loved God. Although I can't remember the class, I do have a vivid memory of lying on my bed at night thinking about *the sentence*. I can still hear my sister's steady breathing across the room. I wished so hard that she would wake up. The fear was in my lungs and made it difficult to breathe. I hated the thought that God was there, an all-seeing, all-knowing, jealous God was there, in the room with me and Liv and this God, the one I was supposed to love more than anyone or anything, was the same God who asked Abraham to murder his son. God was capable of anything.

After a week of lying awake with *the sentence*, I finally confessed to my mother: "Mrs. Y. said we have to love God more than our parents." My mother looked at me and spoke a single word: *"Nonsense."* She was sitting at the kitchen table when she said it, and I was standing very close to her. I can still feel the relief in my chest and a lightness coursing through my body. I turned around, and suddenly weightless, I felt as if I were floating down the stairs to my room.

When my daughter was three years old, she looked up at me and said, "Mom, when I grow up, will I still be Sophie?" I said yes because it's true that a name follows a body over time, but the three-year-old who asked the question bears little resemblance to the grown-up young woman I know today. We need to think of the self as a continuum, a steady story over time. The mind is always searching for similarities, associations, repetitions, because they create meaning. When recognizable repetitions are disrupted, people say, "He wasn't himself," or, "I don't know what came over me. I'm not myself today." A few years ago, I listened to a woman who was both a doctor and a manic-depressive speak in public about a memoir she had written. She described the end of her manic episodes by saying, "I returned to myself." But strictly speaking, that logic is false. Whether people are besieged by a chemical imbalance or thrown into a panic or depression by a wrenching loss, their inconsistencies also belong to the self. It's the feeling or impression of foreignness that makes us want to cast off the interruptions, explosions, lapses, and inconsistencies—all the material in ourselves that we refuse to integrate into a narrative.

I didn't know what to do with what I saw in my mind those nights I lay thinking over the sentence—Abraham's hand clutching the knife and raising it in the air as he prepares to murder his son, to cut open his body. For me, whatever the theological explanation, it was an image of vengeance, rage, and impending mutilation. Many years after that fateful Sunday school class, I sought help from a clinical psychologist at Columbia University, where I was a graduate student. I felt very calm when I walked into Dr. R.'s office, ready to explicate my various troubles and anxieties. I sat down in a chair opposite him, looked him in the eyes, and all at once, without the slightest inner forewarning, burst into tears. He didn't say a word, but I watched his hand move toward a box of Kleenex, conveniently placed within arm's reach, which he then handed over to me. It was a practiced, knowing gesture.

Even at the time, I found a touch of comedy in the scene and wondered how many other distraught graduate students had shed unexpected tears in this doctor's office. It's a sorry little fact that we are often as mysterious to ourselves as we are to others.

I visited Dr. R. for several weeks, but I no longer recall how many. I talked a lot about life and love and my nerves, but there is one comment he made that stands out with the sublime distinctness that only recognition can bring. He said that he thought I was terribly afraid of violence in myself. He then pointed out that he was absolutely convinced that I was incapable of violence either against myself or against anyone else. As soon as the statement was out of his mouth, I felt huge relief. It was as if someone had come along and unloosened a long fat rope that had bound me from neck to toe.

Only in the act of writing this have I understood that Dr. R.'s words echoed the single word my mother had spoken years earlier: "Nonsense."

A field trip to the state hospital in Faribault: The room is large and rectangular, with tall windows that line one of its blank walls. I walk down the aisle between rows of beds. The windows are on my left. A gray light streams through them from outside. I walk slowly and say nothing. Someone, probably the guide, a man or a woman, I don't remember, says that this room is for the "profoundly retarded." In one bed there is a boy, a big child, perhaps ten or eleven, dressed only in diapers wrapped around his slender hips. His hair is dark and silky, and he lies on his back with one cheek turned onto the pillow. The flesh of his thin but flaccid body looks like an infant's—beautiful, white and unmarred. His eyes have no focus. He drools. And then there's a view. I see the parking lot from a distance—three orange school buses in weak sunlight and, behind them, tall and mostly bare trees. I can't say with any certainty whether the view is from inside or outside the asylum, but because I seem to be looking down at the buses, I suspect that I saw it from inside, perhaps from a second-story window. Why that child is fixed inside me is a question I can't fully answer, but I think the sight of him mirrors some speechless fear and sorrow in myself. In him I saw an image of abandonment and isolation greater than anything I have ever seen before or since. And why has the image of the buses stayed with me? Perhaps they were the promise of going home.

One may wonder why the school authorities imagined that trooping ten- and eleven-year-olds through the grim wards of a state hospital would be a beneficial outing. We weren't studying anything that even distantly touched on the subjects of retardation, madness, or state asylums. Our fifth-grade teacher, Mr. L., had certainly not initiated the excursion. (It was probably an annual duty organized by invisible authorities. The following year, we toured a museum dedicated entirely to farm accidents, in which we were treated to life-size models of arms severed by threshing machines and legs mashed in combines.) Mr. L. was young and soft-spoken and respectful. Although I wasn't at all aware of it at the time, I suspect his kindness gave me energy. His classroom was more like my own home, and in that environment I thrived. I wrote, directed, and (selfishly) starred in a play mounted in the school theater; gathered signatures from every pupil in the fifth and sixth grades to petition the principal for the right to talk during lunch (an action that failed miserably); threw myself into writing and illustrating a novel for English called *Carrie at Baxter Manor;* and discovered a passion for the abo-

litionists. I found new heroes in Harriet Tubman and Booker
T. Washington and struggled through the Victorian language
of *Uncle Tom's Cabin*, all the while riding high on a wave of
what children call "popularity."

The following year, my old wound reopened. It began in
February and lasted until the school year ended. For reasons
that were obscure to me, I precipitously fell from favor with
the girls who had once liked me. I turned into a despised
outcast—the butt of cruel jokes and torments. I was jostled,
pinched, and pushed. Every remark I made was met with
snickering and whispers from the girls who by some stroke of
magic had become omnipotent in that tiny world of sixth-
grade pubescent girlhood. I lived in a state of bewildered an-
guish for months. Like most stories of female bullying, mine
began with a single girl. I am sure she had detected my bruised
inner sanctum and took aim. Had I been tougher, I might have
resisted her machinations. She came from a family in which
the sibling rivalry was ferocious. Her desire to hurt me was no
doubt homegrown, but I had few tools at the time for analysis
of her psyche, and even if I had, they probably wouldn't have
done me much good. Open hostility—making sure I was kept
out of games and conversations—mingled with surreptitious
cruelty, false acts of kindness to trick me into believing that I
had been accepted once again. These deceits were worse. The
duplicity sickened me. I drooped and dragged my sorry self
around like a kicked dog. My only defense would have been
genuine indifference. I had seen it in others and would have
loved it for myself, but this quality evaded me. I wanted to be
liked and admired and couldn't fathom what had decided my
abject fate. One day, however, I returned to my desk and found
that a drawing of mine had been marked up and torn. My enemies had made a strategic error. A small breeze of comprehen-

sion blew through me. I was the best artist in my class, and I knew it. My pictures were universally praised, and I was proud of my gift. Desecrating a drawing was a sign of envy.

My visual memories of those months are like gray fragments. I can see the hallway in the school building and the door to the toilet where I would sneak into a stall and shed a few tears as quietly as possible. I remember contemplating my pleated skirt and the gray ribbed wool stockings I often wore in winter as I sat there alone and, despite my unhappiness, felt relieved to be away from the others.

At my mother's urging, my father took up my case with the teacher, Mr. V. That encounter took on mythical dimensions in our family because Mr. V. was surprised by what my father had to say. Oblivious to all the intrigue that had been lurking in his own classroom, he spoke the words my parents would both later repeat to me: "But why Siri? She has so much going for her."

It must have been in November or December of the following academic year that I had an epiphany. I now think that moment was simply a self-conscious recognition of my own dramatically changed circumstances. My family had left Minnesota for Bergen, Norway. My father was spending his sabbatical doing research at the university in the city where my mother's brother and sister and their families lived. I loved the Rudolph Steiner School I attended. I loved my teachers. I loved my best friend, Kristina. The moment came one night after a party given by one of the boys in my class. He came from a wealthy family that lived in a large, low, elegant house outside Bergen. I was wearing the pink dress my mother had sewn for me, a minidress with a lace ruffle down the front,

and the pink suede shoes with a small heel that had been purchased at the largest department store in Bergen. At the party
I had danced with every boy in my class. Each one in turn had
wrapped his arms around me and swayed slowly to the
maudlin class favorite, "Silence Is Golden." As I stepped out
the door into the cold night, I saw that it was snowing. Out-
door lights illuminated the circular drive in front of the house
as well as the snowflakes, which were so large I felt I could see
the articulated form of each one as they fell slowly to the
ground and turned it white. The scene wasn't only beautiful; it
was touched by magic. The dull, brown, and barren world of
only hours before had been transfigured into a new and radiant albescence. I didn't understand it at the time, but no picture could have matched my inner life more perfectly. I told
myself to remember the snow and to remember my pure,
strong happiness at simply being alive to see it. That thought
has never left me.

The lesson of these brutal shifts of fortune ran deep. For
some people, cruelty came easily, shamelessly. For me, every
unkind word I uttered was followed by a merciless guilt and
remorse I could hardly bear. I continue to be preoccupied
with these differences among people. The mysteries of personality aren't easily parsed, but it is certain that human beings run the gamut from the highly empathetic to the
absolutely cold. The secret lies in our bodies and in the stories
of our lives with other people, in the dark nuances of repetitions and interruptions.

*It's the summer of 1968, and most of the day and into the night I
read. I read one book after another. The books excite and agitate
me. I can't stop reading during the day, and for the first time in*

my life I suffer from ongoing insomnia. One night at two o'clock in the morning, I am still awake. I have been reading David Copperfield, *but I've put it down from exhaustion. I get out of bed and walk to the window. I lift aside the shade and look into the night that isn't night but isn't daylight either. A pale yellow-green haze illuminates the rows of houses in front of me. It's Reykjavik in June. There are no people outside and no noises. Everyone is asleep. Standing there, I am struck by a strong but pleasant sadness. All my anxiety leaves me as I look outside. I stand and look for a while longer and then return to bed.*

Again and again, I have seen those houses in that queer light through the window. The memory is stubborn and potent. Why is this memory so insistent when others have vanished? Unlike the evening when I watched the snowfall, I didn't tell myself to remember that view, but it returns to me all the time. The memory carries a feeling of melancholy that is linked to both reading and sleeplessness. The experience of David's childhood had been an enormous one for me. By the time I looked out that window, I had lived through the sadism of Mr. Murdstone, the death of Dearest, the tenderness of button-popping Peggotty, the flinty goodness of Aunt Betsey, and the wonders of Mr. Dick, a character who remains one of my favorites in all of literature. It was that summer I began to nurse the fantasy of becoming a writer. The books made me feel deep and alive, as if these stories were closer to me than anything else. No one could have been less orphaned than I was with my two loving and attentive parents, and yet the sufferings of David Copperfield and Jane Eyre touched on my old sore. I surrendered the whole force of my empathy to the hero and heroine of those novels. Nevertheless, when I read about their sufferings and humiliations, my grief for them was a kind of safe translation—a reinvention of my own emotional life. Through them, I was able to make a turn in myself, and somehow that view from the window seen alone and at night has become an image for what I now recognize as the end of my childhood.

When I say my wound became political in the years that followed, I don't mean that my involvement in the anti-war movement was somehow insincere or that I have any regrets about my activism. As a champion of the downtrodden, the disenfranchised, the poor, and the oppressed, I found a new outlet for the somewhat irrational but nevertheless strong sense I had of being an outsider in a group—uncomfortable, awkward, and quick to feel a slight. Political feeling can't exist without identification, and mine inevitably went to people without power. In contrast, right-wing ideologies often appeal to those who want to link themselves to authority, people for whom the sight of military parades or soldiers marching off to war is aggrandizing, not painful. Inevitably, there is sublimation in politics, too. It becomes an avenue for suppressed aggression and anger, and I was no exception. And so it was that armed with passion and gorged on political history, I became a firebrand at fourteen. For three years, I read and argued and demonstrated. I marched against the Vietnam War, helped print strike T-shirts at Carleton College after the deaths of four students at Kent State, attended rallies, raised money for war-torn Mozambique, signed petitions, licked envelopes for the American Indian Movement, and turned into a feminist.

But even then, I didn't believe all the rhetoric—the puerile drivel that escaped the lips of people like Abby Hoffman and members of the Chicago Seven. The militarism of the Black

Panthers, the violence of the Weathermen, the shallowness of
Guerilla Theater all alienated me. I remember listening to
Russell Means, a leader of AIM, one winter afternoon in Minneapolis as he expounded on the superiority of American Indian culture as if it were a monolith and thinking to myself
that his polemic distorted the vast differences among tribes to
a degree that was nothing short of preposterous. I began to understand that ideologies necessarily push, pull, and tug at reality to make it fit the system. Even when they are committed in
the service of a noble cause, lies inevitably make me recoil.

By the time I entered St. Olaf College as a freshman in the
fall of 1973, the historical period into which I had been swept
had more or less ended. I vividly remember a discussion I had
with a sociology professor my first week as a student. He was
a former priest who had been a civil rights activist and had
marched in Selma. We discussed "the fall of the New Left."

*I am sitting at the bottom of a row of white steps in a narrow
hallway. There is a door with a glass window that leads to
the street. I am sobbing. I was sixteen then and had fallen in
love with a tall, handsome political agitator five years older
than I was. He had ended it. The young women are crouching
on the floor trying to comfort me. It is strange that I don't remember where this took place—except that it must have been
Minneapolis—or who the two people in front of me were. They
weren't close friends, but you would think I could come up with
names or at least what they looked like. I also don't remember
how the romance ended. It seems to me that he had written to
me, but I have no memory of a letter being delivered to that
place. I have repressed it and can't bring it back, no matter how
hard I try. I do know that sitting on those steps, I was incon-*

*solable. My chest heaved. I snorted, honked, and wailed, and the
sheer power of my emotion impressed the two hapless witnesses
to my heartbreak. I could see it in their astonished faces, the features of which are now lost.*

At that moment I was all wound. First loves are often terrible, probably because they are first and there is no conscious
history into which they may be absorbed. And yet, the truth is
I cried *like a baby*, without inhibition or a shred of dignity to
hold me up, and I can't help but feel awed by that weeper on
the stairs. When faced with separation from a person I loved,
I traveled backward into the far reaches of my infancy. I
would fall in love again, and I would suffer separations again,
and I would cry again, but I would never allow myself to sob
with such full-throated, unbridled freedom ever again.

I mourned for a year—the year I again found myself in
Bergen. I was a student at the venerable Katedral Skolen,
founded in the year 1153, and lived outside the city with my
aunt and uncle. My parents had arranged it. Although I didn't
talk much about my sorrow to them, they were deeply aware
of it, and they understood that I needed to be a world away. In
that rainy city of mountains on the western coast of Norway, I
nursed my broken heart, visited my beloved grandmother
every day, read hundreds of books, wrote bad poetry, and
smoked innumerable cigarettes. I was a seventeen-year-old intellectual hermit, and I think it did me good. Not long after I
returned to the United States, the old love object appeared at
my door. I rejected him, and to this day the memory of turn-
ing him away is sweet.

In college I retreated to the library. I have always loved
libraries—the quiet, the smell, the expectation of imminent
discovery. In the next book I will find it—some unspeakable

pleasure or startling revelation or extraordinary nuance I had never felt or thought of before. I sat in the library every day for hours and was happy there, but I hadn't left home. I attended the college where my father was a professor and where he gave many hours of his time to the Norwegian American Historical Association as executive secretary. The association's office was in the college library, and my mother worked in the periodical department of that same library. Two years later, my sister Liv was also studying in that library, and three years after that, my sister Ingrid arrived. Only the third sister, Asti, went away for college to work in another library in another town.

One afternoon, I left my carrel to talk to a male friend who was having a sad bout with a girlfriend. When I returned, I found a note on the desk. It was a letter of remorse. The person who had written it had eavesdropped on me and my friend and discovered that his or her ideas about me had been all wrong. I recall perfectly only this sentence: "I thought you were a cold bitch, but now I know you are a kind, good person." The letter was unsigned. Since I hadn't been aware of this unknown person's dislike for me, I didn't welcome the news, but it didn't surprise me either. By the time I received that letter, I had traveled great distances from the girl in the sixth grade who wept in the toilet, but I was still suspect and was still an outsider. Provincial life feeds on conformity—on the idea that no one should stick out if she can help it. The crippled, retarded, and senile can't help it and are forgiven, but sticking out on purpose was regarded as a criticism of the community at large. Who does she think she is? Indeed, who did I think I was? My twelve-year-old self would have loved to be taken in by her tormenters, but the nineteen-year-old had learned to feel contempt for those who lived by the egalitarian prejudice that ruled my hometown and continued to haunt me through my college years in that same town. And yet the child dreaming in the woods behind the family house, who felt solitary and transcendent and possessed of a singular destiny, remained in the young woman in the library, and perhaps people inhaled that strange, arrogant inner belief and reacted with distaste. If the vulnerable aren't also proud, they are crushed.

I read and I wrote. I wrote stories and poems, far better than the hundreds of pages of awful things I had written in high school. The college literary magazine rejected everything I had to offer. It is interesting to me that I recall those rejections with bitterness but have entirely forgotten other, later rejections. Only a few months ago, I moved my study from one room to another and organized my papers. Among them I found several rejection letters from literary magazines, some of them very long and detailed, which I had no memory of ever having received. It may be that those early dismissals of my writing smacked of personal antipathy, that it hardly mattered what I wrote, whereas the later letters were merely a matter of literary taste. All in all, my inner life with books during college was better than life on campus, and I nurtured vague dreams of leaving Minnesota and its sturdy, sincere, polite Lutherans for somewhere more vivid, more dangerous, more anything.

In the fall of 1975, I signed on for a semester in the Far East. I left home without quite leaving it because the faculty supervisors of the trip were my own parents, and my three sisters came along as well. I was twenty years old, a young woman in a trembling state of readiness for adventure. While a few of my fellow students came down with culture shock, I spent the early weeks of the trip in Japan, Taiwan, and Hong Kong in a feverish trance of pleasure. By the time we arrived in Chiang Mai, Thailand, my body had become so awake to sensual stimuli—to the piercing noises of strange birds, the lilt of Mandarin and Cantonese vowels, colors in the market places so brilliant they almost hurt, the new odors of flowers, the pungent smell of meats, and the stink of unknown fruits— that I felt almost reborn. It is perhaps the only time in my life from which I have no memory of reading anything. I must have read because I took classes, but it couldn't have mattered very much. The words have vanished.

We spent three months in Chiang Mai, and like countless Europeans and Americans before me, I fell under the spell of an eastern enchantment I didn't want to break. It was a form of cultural tipsiness, I suppose, a need to plunge into what I had never seen or tasted before. My years in Norway had been spent with the familiar. I knew the language. My mother's family and my father's relatives lived in that country. In sharp contrast, Thailand was radically foreign. I fell in love with a Thai man, V., and entered a period that on hindsight looks like an explosion of pent-up desire. Every day upon waking I felt it—a wild happiness that surged through me for weeks on end.

My senses remained on high alert, and even thinking back on that time makes me feel giddy. I could never have a similar experience now. I have too much behind me, too many references, stories, too many years of thoughts. I was raw then. Unlike many of my recollections that are weirdly drained of all hues, like a black-and-white movie, my memories of Thailand blaze with color.

I am looking down at the deep brown, wrinkled, and extremely dirty face of a man from one of the hill tribes. He is smiling at me with ochre teeth. His clothes are royal blue and red and covered with silver ornaments that catch the sunlight. In his face I can see that he finds me just as marvelous as I find him.

It is a cool night, and I am standing on the steps of V.'s house when a *tuk-tuk*, one of the small trucks that serve as Chiang Mai's taxis, stops on the road. P. and several others climb out and walk toward us, but it is only P. whom I remember without blur. He is tripping toward me with an enormous grin on his face, dressed in a white T-shirt, narrow blue jeans, and over his shoulders he has draped a brilliant pink feather boa. He stretches out his arms for my embrace and calls out my name: "Sili! Sili!"

V. and I are walking toward the village on a dirt road spotted with pale marks from the sunlight that shines through the dark green trees. Five or six children are walking toward us. One of them is carrying a blaring radio in his arms that blasts out the popular song about Muhammad Ali. I hear the words "dance like a butterfly, sting like a bee." When they get closer, they eye me, begin to shriek, turn, and run fast in the opposite direction. I can see their thin brown legs pumping hard, the dust rising beneath their bare feet. V. turns to me. "They're shouting the Thai word for spirit. They think you're a ghost."

I am watching a small orange lizard on the wall through a gauze of mosquito netting as the afternoon sun shines through the window. The memory is as still as a photograph, and if there was any noise at all, I have forgotten it.

Only the unprotected self can feel joy.

There was another side. I saw two literal wounds during those three months.

The streets are so crowded, it's difficult to move. The whole city has come out for the Festival of Lights. The Mekong River is burning with light from a thousand boats, some tiny, some larger, illuminated by torches and candles. V. and I are walking together, holding hands to keep from being separated by the pushing throng. My sister Asti is somewhere behind me with other friends, and then ahead of me there is a burst of red. Blood. The back of a man. Something has hit his shoulder. The memory is in slow motion, clearly a distortion of what really happened, and yet I watch as the crowd parts, opens onto a view of what? I don't know. People are scrambling away, and V. tugs hard at my arm. There must have been shouting and screaming, but I can't recall these sounds, only add them to the confusion. "Someone threw a Molotov cocktail into the crowd," V. tells me. I still don't know how he knew that. I don't bother to ask. I don't feel anything. I note this. I've seen a terrible thing, and I'm not responding. Was it because I didn't see it well enough? Wasn't it real to me? It's as if I'm anesthetized, absent.

I am near the Burmese border, watching an operation. A young man has been in a motorcycle accident, and his right leg is badly injured. There is blood all over the operating table. I can see the enormous gash in his leg, a messy, deep wound. I am looking down at him and the physicians from a small balcony. Beside me is the doctor with whom I have traveled. I've been living with him, his wife, and his daughter since I arrived in Chiang Mai. I look down at the leg and say to myself, Siri, you are looking down at his injury, and you are okay. You are tougher and stronger than you thought. I silently admire myself. A few seconds later, I feel dizzy. Then the familiar nausea rises up in

my stomach. It has happened before. I feel it coming. My knees
give way, and I'm fainting.

Not long after I returned to the United States, I fell violently
ill. For days, I lay in bed with a head that felt like someone
had left an axe in it. I became a vomiting, shuddering ruin
that couldn't stand upright or tolerate any light from the window. The vertigo and nausea came and went, but the pain in
my head remained in varying forms and degrees for eight
long months. While I sat in the library, dutifully reading
through the pain, I blamed myself for generating a bizarre
psychosomatic symptom, a punishing head that made it hard
to see, hard to read, hard to think—in short, hard to do what I
had to do. But the worst was that as time wore on, I became
more and more afraid of myself, or perhaps more conscious
of the fear I have always had—a fear that within me is some
danger I can't name.

I slowly emerged from the headache and threw myself even
more forcefully into my studies the following year. I became
obsessed with Russian intellectual history—in the nineteenth
and twentieth centuries. It was so vivid, so crazed, so horribly
sad in the end that I filled myself up with it. I continued to eat
books like a starved person. I rejected Jung but was dreaming
for Freud every night, making dreams the master would have
liked: a twenty-year-old woman going through transference
with a dead man. I wrote more poems, composing slowly and
carefully—sonnets. I wrote a lot of sonnets.

It would happen again in 1982. A stupendous headache would
arrive after I had fallen in love, after many months of ecstatic

feeling had reached an aching zenith when I married the man I wanted. The attack began on our honeymoon in Paris with a seizure, one that to my utter astonishment threw me against a wall in the Galerie Maeght and then ended as quickly as it had begun. Half an hour later, I was walking in the street with my husband and my vision suddenly sharpened, as if every building, object, person, and color had been refocused through a powerful camera lens, and then I heard those words in my head, *I have never been so happy in my life as I am now.* I was ill for a whole year. Near the end of that period, I landed in the neurology ward at Mount Sinai Hospital. A listless, prone body that had been ground to a halt by the drug Thorazine, I lay in bed plagued by guilt, busily interpreting my sickness. Had I just imagined I was happy? If I didn't want to be married, why did it seem that I had wanted it so much? I was an enigma to myself, a burden on my new husband, and insane to boot. I have forgiven myself since then. I recognize that migraine can be triggered by any kind of high emotion, be it joy or fear or grief. I am resigned to myself as a jangling, spasmodic, fluttering body that must work to find calm, peace, and rest.

Sometime during my first week in New York City, the week I started graduate school at Columbia University in the fall of 1978, I was standing in the tiny student room I had rented, and I turned to look at myself in the small mirror over the sink. I knew the person I was looking at was myself, and yet there was an alien quality to my reflection, an otherness that brought with it feelings of exuberance and celebration. All at once, I was looking at a stranger. I had left my parents only days before, and when I said good-bye to them at the airport I had felt unexpected tears rise in the corners of my eyes. It seems to me now that in my mirror image I saw a confirmation of my sudden and radical autonomy, a recognition that a cut from home had been made, and I had survived it whole.

I embraced my solitude. I had left everyone I had known and knew nobody in the city. It wasn't long before I cut all ties to the boyfriend I had left in Minnesota as well. I threw him off with the town and my childhood, and I did it abruptly. I still feel bad about it, not because it was a mistake but because in some frightened corner of myself I had known that I would never return to him or include him in my future and had hidden that truth from myself. Years later, I was at a dinner party in New York during which the host loudly declared his undying love for his wife. Two weeks later, he left her for another woman. I am as convinced that his declaration was sincere as I am that he was a cipher to himself.

That fall, I walked into another world. New York City struck me as more brilliant and more alive than anywhere else on earth. My body hummed with the city's speed, verve, and humor. I acquired the urbanite's sixth sense, the ability to detect the vague scent of danger in the streets and stiffen oneself against it. I wore out my shoes walking, and as I walked I rejoiced in the city's massive ugliness, its mysterious ruined blocks, its gorgeous pockets of wealth, its markets, its crowds, its colors. Columbia is in and of the city, and I can't separate one from the other during those years. Both the city and the school were part of a crazy new rhythm of things, a repetitive beat of excitement and discovery. The graduate department in English where I had come to study teemed with critical theory. Foucault, Derrida, Althuser, Lacan, Deleuze, Guattari, and Kristeva were authors I'd never heard of, much less read. By the time I arrived, structuralism had come and gone and the hipsters who populated the graduate schools in the humanities were deep into its postincarnation.

The ideas were our weather. We lived in them and they lived in us, and these hot, strong thoughts cast a subversive glare over Philosophy Hall and the Hungarian Pastry Shop, where students gathered to argue and explain and pick apart the French imports. When Jacques Derrida's latest book was published in English, Salter's, one of the Columbia neighborhood bookstores, posted a large handwritten sign in its window: WE HAVE DERRIDA'S GRAMMATOLOGY! Students stormed the shop to snatch a copy.

Ideas are always personal, too.

I am sitting with K. in the Hungarian Pastry Shop talking to him about Ferdinand de Saussure's Course *in General Linguistics. It's a book K. knows well, and I am asking him about the relation between concept and sound image. He answers me by drawing a small picture of a tree on a napkin. It's similar to an image in the book. I look down at the little drawing and what was abstract becomes real. I understand. A simple lasting revelation: We see through language. The word isolates, defines, creates the borders of the thing. Arbitrary and floating, language dissects the world.*

F. is telling me about Kojève's reading of Hegel. He is a philosophy student, a good teacher, and a dear friend. He is patient, methodical, startlingly articulate. Systems take shape for me in his words. He is talking about the master/slave chapter in The Phenomenology of Mind. *Hegel is too hard on the page, but now I am thinking about self-consciousness, about two-ness, mirrors, about "I"s and "you"s, about entanglement.*

The book is on the library table in front of me. To my left, the windows are letting in the last of the afternoon light that is the beginning of dusk. The book is Roman Jakobson's Two Aspects of Language. *I am reading about aphasia. Jakobson writes that the aphasic patient loses first the words a child learns last— linguistic shifters, like pronouns. I exult in this discovery. I will use it in my dissertation, but more than that I recognize that human identity finds itself only in language as the subject and yet this "I" is fragile; it disappears with the "you." The thought echoes inside me like the articulation of an old, old secret I've always known but never had the words with which to express it.*

I will take some ideas and leave others. It's all a question of resonance. Old thoughts from earlier reading will return in new forms, and I will fall in love with all the ideas that articulate what happens between us, with Martin Buber's *Between Man and Man*, because he investigates the silences of touch and feeling, with Mikhail Bahktin's *The Dialogic Imagination*, because it explicates the raucous plural dance of the novel, and even with parts of the intractable Jacques Lacan, so convoluted and maddening and yet, in some passages, a spark to revelation. In D. W. Winnicott I will find the story of the self and the other, the wounds and the blanks, and how the forgotten back-and-forth of early life becomes who we are. Years later, I will put the insight into the mouth of one of my characters, Violet, in *What I Loved*. "Descartes was wrong," she says. "It's not 'I think, therefore I am.' It's 'I am because you are.'"

I was poor in the city, and when I read, wrote poems, or just lay awake in my apartment I heard my neighbors through the thin walls. They rattled their pots and pans when they cooked, argued with one another, and made noisy love. Police sirens, rumbling garbage trucks, footsteps in the hallway made me jump and then kept me vigilant for the next sound. A young woman was raped in the elevator of my building. I heard stories of muggings, senseless attacks, and murders. One night on my way home, an ordinary-looking man stopped me on the street. I thought he wanted the time, but instead he lunged at me with a livid face and barked out an obscenity before I managed to duck and run. Men pursued me hard in those days, and there were times when I felt emotionally assaulted. They were too hungry, too eager, too full of lust I couldn't return, and after an evening out I could feel depleted by their stubborn, never-ending pressure. Then it was a relief to be alone, a relief to see my books, my typewriter, my bed. And yet it was a time of dancing, too, of late nights and sporadic, short-lived passions I pursued on my own terms. My own aggression pleased me. But I wanted K., perhaps because he wanted me only fitfully, because he was elusive. I fell into and then got caught in the repetitive machinery of perverse desire—happiness and pain at regular, then predictable intervals, the cycles of an idiot in love—and finally, after many months of motion, the engine ground to a halt. I didn't want it anymore.

February 23, 1981. I am leaving the reading with J., and we pause in the lobby of the 92nd Street Y to talk about the poems we have just heard. From where I am standing I notice a beautiful man in front of the door. He has a slender face, enormous eyes, and a small, delicate mouth. His hair is nearly black, and his skin is pale brown. He is smoking a little cigar, and he hunches over in his leather jacket and blue jeans as he brings the reed of tobacco to his lips. I notice that his feet are rather large, and I like these big feet, too. In seconds, I have taken in the whole of him and feel woozy with attraction. I can't remem-

ber if J. sees me ogling and tells me that he knows the man or if I ask him if he has any idea who that person is. "That's Paul Auster," he says, "the poet." We are introduced, and then the three of us head downtown in a taxi. In the backseat, Paul tells me about George Oppen, the poet he has just visited in California. I like his voice, and I like the warmth, the tenderness, I hear in it when he speaks of "George." I didn't think it then, but now I wonder if I wasn't hearing something familiar. My father had that when he was alive. He was alive then. My father's voice changed inflection when he spoke about someone he loved. In the taxi, I am already in love, crazed, enthralled, smitten, and am trying to hide it. The man beside me is not. I can see it in his shrouded, thoughtful eyes. I don't let him go. At the party, I talk only to him. We eat. We talk. We walk in the streets and talk. We sit in a bar and talk. The beautiful eyes are gaining focus. He is looking at me, listening to me. I can tell that he likes me.

It is early in the morning and we are standing on West Broadway together in the street. I am standing very close to him, looking into his face, but now, after hours and hours of talk, I have nothing to say. It is late. The evening is over, and I will go home and think about him. Then he kisses me, and it's the best kiss in the world. A cab pulls up and we climb in together.

Not long after that, I read his poems, his essays, and finally the first half of The Invention of Solitude, "Portrait of an Invisible Man." There were many books inside me by then, and yet these jolted me with their originality. I met the man before I read what he had written, but if I had not loved his work as I did or if he had not admired my writing, it would have changed things. Our work has been an intimate part of our love affair and marriage for twenty-three years, but what I read wasn't then and isn't now what I *know* when I'm with him. His work comes from the place in him I can't know.

"When I get stuck," Professor S. said to me, "I do automatic writing like the Surrealists. Try it." S. was one of my professors at Columbia and a poet I admired. I was stuck. I had written many poems since I arrived in New York two years earlier but had rejected most of them as derivative or just weak. When I finally produced a poem I liked, I sent it out to *The Paris Review,* and to my astonishment, the poem was accepted and published. And yet, by the time I spoke to S., my work had begun to harden with self-consciousness, as though some inexorable pressure were bearing down on it. I hated my own words. That night I took S.'s advice and sat down at my blue typewriter in my apartment on 109th Street and wrote freely, and as I wrote I remembered what I had forgotten. I remembered the yellow paper my father gave his girls when he took us to the Historical Association, where he would work at his desk as we drew on the floor. Family stories came back to me—the bits and pieces of the life I had left. I noticed patterns, repetitions—a form emerged that I could never have invented beforehand. Something had broken in me, and I was writing like a person possessed. By the time I went to sleep, I had poured out thirty pages. For three months I edited and reedited those thirty pages into a prose poem. It was the best thing I had ever done.

After that, I never wrote anything in lines again. It would all be prose, and the best prose would always come in a flood. Where does the need to write come from? What is it? It is a need, not a choice. It's a giving way and a giving up. I remember finding a reference to hypergraphia in a book on the nervous system. The obsessive need to write for hours and hours every day, the author said, was sometimes a symptom of epilepsy, linked to a pathological condition in the brain's left temporal lobe. Auras. Fits. Writing. Dostoyevsky had it. Saint Theresa probably had it. My husband has often said, "Writing is a sickness." But many people who aren't epileptics have the need to write for hours and hours every day. Could my need to write be connected to my neurological sensitivity? Maybe, but not *what* I write. Content is what few neurologists discuss.

I am afraid of writing, too, because when I write I am always moving toward the unarticulated, the dangerous, the place where the walls don't hold. I don't know what's there, but I'm pulled toward it. Is the wounded self the writing self? Is the writing self an answer to the wounded self? Perhaps that is more accurate. The wound is static, a given. The writing self is multiple and elastic, and it circles the wound. Over time, I have become more aware of the fact that I must try not to cover that speechless, hurt core, that I must fight my dread of the mess and violence that are also there. I have to write the fear. The writing self is restless and searching, and it listens for voices. Where do they come from, these chatterers who talk to me before I fall asleep? My characters. I am making them and not making them, like people in my dreams. They discuss, fight, laugh, yell, and weep. I was very young when I first heard the story of the exorcism Jesus performs on a possessed man. When Jesus talks to the demon inside the man and asks for his name, the words he cries out both scared and thrilled me. The demon says: "My name is Legion." That is my name, too.

2004

SIRI HUSTVEDT

The Blindfold

'Iris Vegan is a graduate student at Columbia University in New York whose vivid encounters with a series of strange and sometimes nameless characters are powerful enough to convince the reader that the world previously seen as normal has ceased to exist . . . Gripping . . . A complex exploration of the nature of the self, executed in polished and immediate prose'
The Times

'Brilliant . . . a dark, mesmerising debut'
Independent on Sunday

'Hustvedt has pulled off nothing less than a re-mapping of the modern feminist psyche . . . The quality and spareness of her prose, the intensity of her imagination, are at work on one of the most macabre terrains of the 20th century – New York'
Daily Telegraph

'It has vivid and compelling characters; it is scary, sinister and readable . . . a very smart novel'
Independent

'Sexy without being steamy, intelligent without being complicated'
New Statesman

'A work of dizzying intensity – completely urban and modern . . . an intriguing and sure-handed debut by a writer of eloquent and vivid disposition'
Don DeLillo

'A haunting first novel . . . An impressive debut'
Sunday Express

'Hustvedt's descriptions of the city and its manners are as amusing and polished as those of a practised essayist'
Observer

SCEPTRE